I0272334

Peter Hughes was born in Oxford in 1956, and now lives on the Norfolk coast, with his wife Lynn, in a coastguard cottage which is creeping ever closer to the cliff edge. His first publication was in 1983, since when a number of chapbooks and pamphlets have appeared, as well as a Selected Poems, *Blueroads*, from Salt (2003), and two full-length collections from Shearsman Books: *Nistanimera* (2007) and *The Summer of Agios Dimitrios* (2009). Peter Hughes is also the editor/publisher of Oystercatcher Press, which publishes a number of chapbooks every year, and which won the inaugural Michael Marks Award in 2009.

Born in 1960, Simon Marsh moved to Milan in 1984. In 2008, he left the city for the village of Valverde in the Oltrepò Pavese. He now lives in the nearby town of Varzi.

In addition to poetry, he writes and performs music with a group based in Milan. His published works include *Bar Magenta* with Peter Hughes (Many Press), *The Ice Glossaries* (Poetical Histories), and *The Vinyl Hat Years* (Tack/Many Press).

The Pistol Tree Poems

How sweet it is when mother Fancy rocks

Peter Hughes
&
Simon Marsh

Shearsman Books

First published in the United Kingdom in 2011 by
Shearsman Books
50 Westons Hill Drive
Emersons Green
Bristol
BS16 7DF

www.shearsman.com

ISBN 978-1-84861-171-9

Acknowledgements
Some of these poems first appeared as a Kore broadsheet & in *Shearsman* magazine, *Holly White, Unarmed Journal* and *Upstairs at Duroc.*

Special thanks go to Peter Philpott & his *Great Works* for outstanding hospitality.

The Pistol Tree Poems

1

this morning I'm listening to a little country music
by Schubert & liaising with the weather—
the naked sun did lift the sky but then it rained
& now it's putty & porridge cloud
dragging everybody's heaven to Leicester
ignoring my plans to mow the lawn
& plant some wild sweet pea seeds
under the gloomiest section of holly
where Schubert has finally arrived too
did you manage to plant your rhubarb?
I think it needs a well-manured soil
& a little chimney to grow in
so it doesn't get smoke in its eyes
but grows long & firm in the dark
not like a shrivelled penis in the North Sea
teaching phonics to KS1 for £9 a year
didn't make Schubert very exhuberant
nor did beer with Mayrhofer
the poet who eventually threw himself out of
the government building where he worked
as a censor: talk about performance management
what grim times for artists & citizens
the public interested only in dance fads
& minor celebrities sucking each other's faces
Metternich kicking out Joseph II's reforms
banning controversial t-shirts in the capital
abolishing trial by jury in certain cases
5 years in prison for breaking an ASBO
over 3 million DNA samples held on file
damaging GM crops defined as terrorism
the Anti-Terrorism Acts making it an offence
to advocate the violent overthrow of dictators
your internet history available
to entire herds of minor government voyeurs
citizens extradited to America with no evidence
profiles of 37% of black men held by police
peace campaigners prosecuted for causing
US servicemen "harassment, alarm & distress"
by holding a sign outside an American base

saying GEORGE W. BUSH? OH DEAR
here the rain it raineth every day
even now in early May
but Berlusconi has been shown a door   vero?
Schubert was soon into deep mid-winter
I have done nothing wrong
that I should shun mankind
the road I have to take
has always been a one-way street
I heard a cuckoo at 6.15 this morning
& the house martins are back & building
the sun is trying to see us all again
for the cup final & rhubarb
is shaping to wave goodbye to this grey sky

May 2006   Norfolk

2

The sky over the Po Valley reads like a Bisto pack;
it's a duff way to pay the rent:
describing the describable,
and yet I've watched these hills for days and nights,
caught up in an infinitesimal part
of this huge tectonic sigh.
Once grounded, the rain's designated path is a slew
of mud and road-strewn stones,
each taken so far then gripped,
nudged against unevenness;
too much friction is something to hold fast to:
much in the way that Mrs. Pina's goat
is more an extension of herself,
even when, dizzy and drawn by illusions of freedom,
it bolts down the wet hill at gusty dawn
while due to leverage and tree-root shift,
the entire garden sways, imperceptibly plied
for an instant, ever so slightly from sloped earth.
It's perhaps because there's only so much slack
to take up at any given time
that what remains flaps free:
a soft awning of Ligurian wind,
which billows deeply sifted,
somehow leaves colours of the inter-tidal zone
mixed with tree leaf and shadow, and Rhubarb?
Rheums tube their 'neathward way hereabouts,
but on the surface? Nothing.
In search of a remedy,
I side-scroll the OS map, reshuffle whole counties
and select a corner of the Rhubarb Triangle,
which gets dragged south to Valverde,
accompanied by the idiophonic metal ping
of a successfully concluded desktop event:
distant pickers grope dim forcing sheds and emerge,
heroic and blinded by searing hill light,
to the hypnotic film score tones of octet for rhubarb,
                                        goat,
                        virtual jukebox,
          aching root,

petioles,
found objects,
soul-lack
and Prepared Triangle.
Somewhere between Liszt
and the Ottoman marching bands
dwelt the as yet unfelt, explicit
valvey hoof-click
of the bebop scale, and
Steve Reich's audient knitting:
a holding pattern; purl one,
a lossless,
ectopic
beat.

June 2006 Valverde / Milan

3

edging the lawn with worn long-handled shears
just above sea level   it's hard to understand why maps don't tally
with what we're walking up & down on
or why what's in the papers doesn't chime with anyone we know
& why of two rhubarb plants
the first should unfurl & rise like a magic Arabian tent
all high red poles & voluminous masses of cool green shade
whispering spices   while the second is barely alive
should we dig it up & replace it with ginger & a few ears of wheat?
measuring the garden for new fencing
the figures change strangely depending
on which end I start from—
it's impossible to get your bearings   futile & indispensable to try
I wonder if Heine's last note ever got to Camille?
a perfect fix will give only an impossible point
to dance upon: a cocked hat at least gives a small
badly-prepared triangle to cultivate & live in
where a robin flits through a white poplar
& an arpeggio of goldfinches veers into the birches
as for courses to steer
what with all these uncertainties of tidal stream & weather
boat speed & appetite   cross track error
horizontal dilution of precision   still   steer we do
I'd even choose rope not for its qualities of strength
knot & give   but with reference to our shared cack-handedness:
polypropylene makes a poor enough rope
but at least it floats when you misjudge & drop it
down the crack between some country or other
& the side of your dilapidated boat -
& it'll still stop the goat going off-piste for a go at
the artichokes   herb garden   or other goat
tonight I'd rather navigate like the Polynesians once did
imagining position from the sway
& underlying tendency of the waves
while assembling lyric maps which trace the shapes
made by the clearest of these clear stars
                                        the Plough upended on The Wash
                        Scorpius gradually wheeling past the back garden
using bits of driftwood   seaweed   flotsam   finger marks

reflecting on a change in the weather & unusual sea level
Schumann on the radio paints in some extra sand-banks
for the oystercatchers & seals   & Heine's Fly
I often put in yellow instead of blue
& recall Buy Ballot's Law:
the low pressure area should be on your left
if you stand with your back to the wind
the house martins fussed & keened & banked all evening
till the light slid off the edges of the sea & land
in the hours after dark you can feel them
   tucked up under the eaves of the house
                    you can feel them breathing
as the tide quietly rocks towards the moon they're watching

June 2006   Norfolk

4

What B.B. sought to calibrate on the train
– was it from, or to Utrecht? –
might have been a wolf note:
the jute sack with the brass suppressors
slouched forgotten on platform 2,
a stop trick, and it was gone:
as if drawn through a fantascope of melodeon air
less than a sheng hoot away!
I never could say sphygmomanometer
quick enough to work   the magic spell;
the diamond mirror turned on yourself,
to free you from Armide's
                                        caresses
the witch's g-string hummed, alright:
a mad flash of panties
and Clorinda was as if long forgotten:
caught up between love itself
and a sort of seasonal pitch shift
            in the atria of the heart.
What if your rope were wound with tarred hemp?
Paid out from the barque,
            from the Wash to the Oltrepò
there's not much knicker in Delacroix,
but there are boats; in Dieppe, for instance,
where the waves' dark pleats
are like ruffled coal.
A mooring hitch; a rough-hewn cleat,
pack your astrolabe
and stuff the hold with Heinz:
one tin for each navigational star,
sit back and sense
the ocean's swell,
where serpent stars fade
tangled into   day.
Dawn said Charlie Chestnut *Is the crack between worlds.*
And if we dropped the rope right there?
The copper core feeding uploaded Pistols
onto the sharp rim
of earth's perceptible curve.

You can't cull lunes from accessory fruit,
but you can make rhubarb crumble,
or lace the cornstarch base
with local hooch
to put hairs back on your shirt.
Slipping down through these hills can be imperceptible,
or like getting out of bed on an achy morning;
oncoming cars hurl themselves into bends
in a massive display of serial wanking
and poppies cheat last light
at the road's edge:
crimson shadow-hearted folds
clutch the sun's cruel retainer.

June/July 2006   Valverde / Milan

5

if I could only clear my desk of goats
notes & rhubarbarian hooliganism—
at least I've learned that goats have preorbital vacuities
& so does the fundamentalist gonging on
on the radio   impersonating a dalek in a popemobile
how shall we tell the sheep from the goats? he creaks
how about goats have 60 chromosomes not 54
a little beard they hold their tails up & look a lot like fucking goats
          the continent takes so long to drag itself sideways
the speed of our fingernails growing   or oil paint drying
          in the subduction zone the floor disappears
locality transformed into possibility
yet according to the King's Lynn Tide Tables
it's still 2290 sea miles to La Spezia
on the journey swallow certain details of the planet's surface: first catch your rhubarb
& get your left hand down among its little crotches   give one stem a savage
leg-break tweak then do 5 more completing the over cart your flappy booty to
the end of the garden & strip off the leaves for organic pesticide when boiled with
2 litres of water (or just boil the pests) or a satisfying tea when brewed with 200 mil
for the man on the radio   ignore the classical smalls on the line bad for the
blood pressure   back in the kitchen manoeuvre your curved length under a
cold tap 3 times then turn the tap on so water celebrates all over this crisp & bitter
structure then chop it up to rhubarb-size chunks with a light knife that will stop
against anything stringy prompting you to raise the offending baton to edge back
the superficial by alternating pushes of the still-articulated sections   transfer to
your worst saucepan with a lisp of fresh water   a whisper of sugar   & a wish of
cinnamon & ginger stir with attractive wooden paddle-shaped implement over a low
heat & a bluesy background like Zucchero's *She's My Baby* when the bridge kicks in
again turn the heat up without warning for 20 seconds & flick in a spit of white wine
turn heat back down for next track to
reassure rhubarb then get some Greek yoghurt blob this into the syrupy juices all
tangy & translucent with a pollen of freshly-grated nutmeg seven little hedgerow
berries & an icing of vodka breath straight from the expiring freezer & that is actually
the goat
looking in through the kitchen window   what or whom is it standing on?
a pile of papers ready for recycling a million words on athlete's foot & string theory
new food   frocks & hybrid skateboards
if an atom were a solar system a string would be a tree
under the tree the guests are fleeing as Typhon tries to crash the party

almost everyone runs & manages to turn into an animal   except Pan
who plunging into the river   only does the job by halves   underwater he's all fish-tail
above he still plays the goat   Zeus laughs his rocks off
& nails Capricornus up beyond the sycamore forever   mind you
Typhon's still banged up under Etna   stuck inside his chimney   we've all been there
the stars shine down on the papers & mint   my nephew's buggy abandoned
after he's betrayed by heat   heart   &   midsummer afternoons:
a light summer drizzle filters the sun & Sam sees a bee in a flower in the rain
he cups it in his hands   nursing it towards the shelter of the house & cries out as it
stings deep in his tender palm   do you recall your own key innoculations?
our fashionable goat is thrilled by recent DEFRA guidance:
if you applied a tattoo before 9th July 2005   that you can no longer read
you can replace it with another tattoo
now I'm making this compress for stings from nettles & desktop-clutter
say the sideways-moving jaws of the face with the goatee

Cambridge   July 2006

6

A glass of chilled Gavi after the morning sauna
has the same effect as a dollop of cranberry jelly in your draught lager
and now I am haunted by imaginary German words for mystical fish.
I should never have summoned the witch in N°.4,
she came to me in dream two nights ago
so I let the earth's once spin shake off and compact what I recall:
did she really force mauve felt plums into my mouth?
Tall enough to hook my neck in her elbow pit
and draw me in from a deep, long lonely sense of touchlessness;
the passage from powder shade to wan moonlight
and the quivering tenderness I have sought so long.
I found my tattered Byron Foot Club membership card
in this frock coat pocket
only it was my knee, the magnetic resonance said,
And the *referto* was Clorinda's heart, made out of iron-filings on the
whitest paper.
I stood in front of an unfinished house on the side of a freeze-frame hill;
a cement mixer abandoned in the grassless yard:
A probe fallen
clumsily
to earth.
But now I'm back on my old Claud Butler again,
back rim still slightly buckled
from the legendary Ramsgate harbour fall
brought on by the heavy bar room malady of unrequited love
and one too many pinch bolts bartered for draught Spitfire.
The irregular wheel transmits a wobbly pulse
and at every pedal push
the sun draws more visible light toward one last point,
which if you think that
pulleys and lines are weightless
no energy is lost due to friction
lines, supposedly, do not stretch
and the total force on the pulley must be zero
probably means I'm slowly winching another day off its own edge
though with no block and tackle in sight to speak of.
Then the sun bobs upwards behind cloud,
leaving the fishmonger's window somewhere between splatter
and pollack by Pollock.

Kids on the passing tram fry their brains with rap
            –I'd swear one's shouldering a jute sack–
and was that a goat or the space cowboy at the filthy window?
Typhon and Pan are arguing with the ticket inspector
'cause we ain't got DEFRA pet guidelines on Milano ATM,
where a hunting dog is a *what is it doing or what is it for* question.
Rail side tree lymph clogs at the base
and brittle-tipped, limp leaves are a sure sign
That root creak   has set in
and like it or not they're in the loop
of what we have to hand,
which is not so much carelessness as uncaring:
and constantly on the threshold of how outspoken that can be

Valverde / Milan   July 2006

7

from a rusting garden deck-chair I sense bats cavort & squeak
extra satellites of love roll overhead   forging the future
grain & powder whisper censored secrets in dark & concave steel
things go round & round   echoing   in & out & in the head
I lost my way with words for those few years   reaching rock bottom
& virtual dyslexia when I turned up at Claud's toga party as a goat
the worst of Tasso is maybe the best at any time of personal crisis
so any time really   Torky said: I'll make up lovely bits
so we can cope without heroin   when history slams us back
              against the wall
that modest flat in Beirut   have you any idea of what it took?
shifts in stars & bucks helping to trade adverts for animal skins
& oil from the plains to make the deposit   *blauaurenfisch*
                              Aladine (Sid James) is trolling about on the battlements
with his hands stuffed up his sleeves   & a moustache that comes off
               in the rain
while Rinaldo hides his red card   & lives out a 3-match ban watching DVDs
of Bush & Blair roasting Armide for her own good
Ismen said the conquest of Jerusalem would always be temporary
dig your nails into your own palms   what's the writing about?
& Monteverdi & Rossini can coexist   thank you Melvin
          when I bring on the mirror guys   pretend to be self-aware
these bloody goats you lent me   have upset 8 sets of neighbours
I hitched them to the washing line so they could run up & down the garden
but they found that by working together they could give each other a bunk-up
into next door   this could cost me more than your damn holiday
in Disneyland   what with all their salad-crops cropped to earth
towers of ant-ridden artichokes trampled underfoot
enormous sweet potatoes reduced to chiselled radishes   their legs-in-the-air
rhubarb-leaf
oxylic acid highs   & where the blues comes from is: the G-string always will unravel
wound or unwound   it will always spoil your D chords
(as though they were any different from anyone else's)
         this is where the words of others grow   walking the dog
         brushing against the backs of your hands like growing oats
   breathing in & out like the pre-dawn estuary waters wearing boats
here in the level meadows watered by snowmelt from neighbouring countries
the story crosses & recrosses the low plains of our private embarrassments
with a suggestion of ¾ time   haunting the broad meanders

we've come to a temporary settlement   there's all to negotiate
we came along back lanes   down this track to the allotments
how about: after harvest festival I get your bicycle you get my goat
I never really mastered the serenade
in spite of rubbing many instruments up the wrong way
shouldering these bagpipes Clorinda   & inflating the scrotum & garters
& non-existent moustache
I go back to those heady days of day-long head
not to mention the thrush banging a snail on the end of your dick
when daylight or darkness were evensong enough
those days are these & we are living them with the things of this world
& in the multiscreen complexes of our hearts: plunge your hand again
into this popcorn box from which I've cunningly removed the base
the lights dim   coughing dies   music starts   gently

Winchester / Oxford / Cambridge July 2006

8

From this height, lakes appear like cobalt rips scuffed with wind
cloud is too white to be cauliflower, but those teeny glints of green light
could be distant rheums a sway in some-man's land, or else a trick of the bent breeze,
the hills pushed up from 'neath knuckles pressed into some pre-birth membrane
force ribbing, which is outlined by the darkest ever slabs of shadow
the sky from above makes no real sense
and you don't see many Turnstones at 38,000 feet
still a momentary misalignment of the beak, a wing beat too many
could be enough to gain these scarce, near-airless frozen outsides
beyond the fuselage-boom, where tiny ice cubes jingle
wring the chillier bits of Glass
                    from frozen ornithological scrota.
I think you once told me that the Purple OysterCatcher played alto with Sun Ra
it's funny how birds' names describe what they do:
I might've been called Shagbestfriendssister, or Didntgeteminalot
Lancelot, like Tarky, knew that every epic needs
                              its Guinevere
                                        and a good dose of helmet.
All this time the sun is perched more or less to the west, the plane Dutch rolls
imaginary corridors,
and I gaze down at the Frenchness of carpet sampler beige crop rotation,
not knowing   where I am   or what time it is
the undercarriage sounds like a jeweller's drill, but feels like the opening
sequence of a Bond movie
and though I could sway all day in these gusts of wind, I end up on the train heading
south
Battersea Power station protruding like a primitive multi-pin connector
an auxiliary to a potentially unlit London, where I never stop, but burrow across or
bounce off
and get welcomed to Margate Main Sands—*deckchairs and sun beds for your pleasure*—
where blonde tarts in minis in Minis double decrutch the Golden Mile
—*help keep our beaches clean and safe: only leave your footprints*—
and there's a strong sense of unkindness in the air, of low-tide kelp,
so I ride the Thanet Loop all day, flip past double-lined, Old Town streets
undulating over bulging Victorian sewers, an' Bev an' Trace an' Shaz
an' the Birdsfoot Trefoil freeze their nipples off down Broadstairs,
where teens e-flirt on Samsungs and there's all day breakfast in Mr. Chips,
and—*have you paid and displayed*—like the vaguely inter-tidal upskirt wench at the
back of the bus

they say half of them would if you knew how to ask
which makes me an old dog and these are old dog whelk tricks Mr. Savoy Sausage, Mr. Hake in Batter, Missed her by the end of the week
slumped back into an Estuary English which is not my own
living for days on goat's milk and Shreddies and the occasional pint of IPA in the Lord Nelson
where they still play Mott The Hoople, though it's Hendrix in The Shakespeare
and The Isle itself scares me somewhat: being here alone again, oh Caged Heart.
Above Botany Bay gulls still rise vertically into view
hover never motionless
against near-visible wind
which conveys cartoon cheese-whiff trails of hobbling squeeze box tuplets
from distant Folk Week prancers,
the Morris Squire's got bells on and is a bit of a tool
thinks the seated woman, who smokes
haggard in the first floor bay window
and never taps her foot

August/September 2006 Thanet–Milan

9

these muggy nights put the mockers on sleep
stew dream to sweaty clods of nonsense:
a late long call from Barry MacSweeney via satellite
slurring some half-roasted thoughts on a bright new range of soft drinks
then interference phased out to absolute clarity
somewhere between the cool voice of Pearl on the high fells
& the sticky pearl necklaces of Jury Vet
Ba dubbed Newcastle tango onto Walk the Line
    the real phone rang with silence packed into the other end
I reached a hand down to crab a feel under the bed
for my glasses & found instead
the clutter of the past packed in the dark
a long box of fireworks   now exotic names & smells
instructions   dusty leakage   dense buff hamstrung jumping jacks
volcanic cardboard cones   squat tubs of vacant flash & stench
the empty sky after the flares was always darker than before
next to the fireworks a tight white box
with brass-hinged lid containing delicate rosary beads
Dinky toys   blue plastic lead from a lost toy dog
the hot fists of a great live bonfire   that mad red cage at your face
rocking in its own evisceration   silhouetting your own hair
but then we each walked away through a range of endless open doors
annotated calendars rolled up to fit the bin
dead bonfire   bleached tins   tremulous ash   archaeological hush
I should patch up no. 7 where something has chewed holes in the text
instead I jam along with music for guitar & harp from Mali
& realise that Frank O'Hara's greatest influence was Louis Armstrong
straddling that hectic knife-edged urban whirl
with a lippy rhythmic mastery affecting nonchalance & kites
but powered by a V8 bolted to the floor under a tablecloth by Miró
I remember when Miró pulled rope into his pictures for the first time
& I wish I could send him one made out of kevlar
up which I pull myself back into the present where the drought reveals
the outlines of another house overlapping our own
a house that was never built but shows where we might have lived
a chunk of the house martins' nest just crumbled away
leaving two chicks dead on the oil-stained drive
but all the other birds are well & set to fly into the rest of our lives
Lynn shouts out suggestions for the poem: *what about*

Paddy McGinty's Goat   she says *or slingbacks*   *that's a good word*
she's not wrong   thanks Lynn   even though I only have a few lines left
& a nearly empty bottle of *Goats Do Roam* too near the mouse
so I move it a span to the right but now my mind's clogged
with Byron's odour-eaters   root-creak embrocation
the network of darkness woven inside   look up
sometimes the sense of death makes you feel more alive
like a jet of warm lemon juice straight on the tongue
from the fruit still heavy with afternoon sun
the end of *Goat's Head Soup* Ba: *Can You Hear the Music*   *Starre Starre*

September 2006   Cambridge

10

(or how goats get their oats)

Around about that time (it was the time of the Mortadella Man, Dearly Beloved) Aikin' Bum and Lil' Fucker were strolling down a bent country road when they come across The Third Billy Goat Gruff, [POV Shot] who's sitting outside a sort of Tracey Emin beach hut, knocking back Draughtflow Body with Brer Rabbit and Brer Fox and pouring his heart out about some family hassle with a Scandinavian *punkabestia*. *–Have a crisp–* says Brer Fox, *–Ta Baby–* replies Brer Rabbit, and seeing Aikin' & Lil', Brer Fox plot dumps the scene where BGG_3, tired of the stench of boiled brethren, hooks a hind hoof into the soft foothill, whips out a Rocket Powered Recoilless Weapon and, bleating a Vin Diesel one liner *–you can flog a dead horse, but you can't make it drink–* sends Sodaroundalot, the one-shot Troll, to meet his maker, who turns out to be a sockpuppet astroturfer (in reality, the Troll himself) high on glory holes and scopofilia *–the way she stoops; tightens her things–* [Gaze Shot: Dita Von Teese look-alike in Pierre Mantouxs, mauve astrodocs, wild silk thimble gloves]. All this time Aikin' & Lil' are booty popping to some *New Groove* and the mid-distant, waiting Wolf is sucking pensively on a lump of chalk, nursing the hurt and wondering why wolves always get so much shit in fairy tales. So I ask him about Mirò and rope and why there aren't any furry handcuffs in Schiele and whether the weather's thick lid really does contain the steamy howl of one huge hump

—Puss in Boots— lisps the wolf

—her lip gloss stings the air with fruit pulp embedded with chrome shards; her storm-hewn eyelids are powder kegs. I used to tense at the sound of brittle hooves rattling; at the thin bleating of a faithless heart, but I've since lost vast tracts of my youth: I remember a pig pen and a git on stilts, a reeking sow, a sausage in a sling, breeze block six-packs heaped at the edge of the open maw. What was it had fell to earth, made this great hole, trashed the snipped lawn bower behind the bus shelter?-

–Tempo da lupi– I reply *–wolf weather—*

the frottoir zips, unzips Acadian off-beats

whisk broom spanked
[why not? grins the Witch]
as Boozoo Chavis tugs at the dance of the
Rougarou

Valverde / Milan 2006

11

(tetley bondage issue)

my range of sex toys based on Miró sculpture
proved an unexpected flop even with a tempting *prendi tre*
paghi due (& free Duracell battery / mains adaptor) offer
launched in six charcoal designer hotels in Milan you could've blown me
down with the *Alien Maid's Kit* oscillating feather duster
I was sure that Europe's finest would've jumped
at the chance of being shafted by art for cash it would've
added such a piquant symmetry to the last few hundred years
& what a Must-Have Gift or Souvenir from your City-Break
in Barcelona (although you only went early Christmas
shopping in Leeds) they could even go in the dishwasher
providing a bit of extra agitation to beat those baked-on
Saturday night stains that won't come off with Mr Muscle
my money spent I heat up the last of the leek & rabbit soup
the temperature's dropped it's The World at One:
there isn't an empty cell in the kingdom
so as a compromise between imprisonment—
which we know to be effective—& community service
(which is underused & could save Councils millions
solving the current shortage of Nursery Assistants
& Poets in Prisons) as from next spring criminals will have
their feet set in blocks of concrete & will be threaded onto
long lines of wire to constitute boundaries for civic events
Cup Finals Royal Commemorations & those places
where they wire up monkeys to stop them wanking in zoos
with two layers all around the Ian Paisley Peace Park
repeat offenders will rope off new organic cod farms too
it's all going to be very exciting—said a spokesman—& in cities
they can be bollards & clean your windscreen at the same time
sometimes a chunk of land covered in dense tufts of grass
gets separated from the coastline: a little floating island
I sometimes feel I've been on one for ages Andy
[Extreme Long Shot] ambiguous time conveyed by dissolves
& superimpositions I can cut the grass with nail scissors
& paddle my lawn wherever my fancy takes me
from Orkney to Livorno & even up the Po
there might be somebody buried in my craft

pushing up daisies & rhubarb & providing ballast
discover who   in the next exciting episode in which
I get to the point where I'm walking down an airport corridor
only to be overtaken by myself   riding one of those
conveyer belts that remind me of the flow of the Tiber
below the Broken Bridge in Rome   we're back to pulse & tone
& dying for another taste of Boozoo Hoodoo live at the Habibi temple
who stole my monkey   down home on dog hill I pull the string
on *der grosse Drachenkopf* kite which goes way over my head
it's such an insubstantial footing out here on the autumn saltmarsh
I want to play with your poodle

Cambridge – Norfolk 2006

12

Did I ever tell you about Evangeline?
She took me on day trips to Plankton
replete with crab line and shrimp net.
While she sunned in her
thigh-long pink print frock
I watched the Witch hitch sodden skirts
way off beneath the tide line
to hook rubbery, hard-shelled aliens
from tiny, countersunk arseholes in the sand.
One day
I'm struggling with the real implications of what is actually on TV
Evangeline
leans on the sill
sorts her knickers with a swift pinch
says something like:
—see how the city fills
bleeds vulnerability
as close as you will ever get to rare beauty,
set all other forms of life aside
feel the words run
through you
then run you through—
Evangeline
was so Gerry Anderson
she tightened her boots
with a hex head wrench
passed groomed, dark nights in velour catsuit and purple crepax wig
stalking Sodaroundalot and his foul-mouthed cuz, Ascending Remus
I fumbled with her utility belt
fished for wayward pouting off the groin
I know now that I was hopelessly drawn
we played backgammon
[*—I'm a hog for you, baby—* hissed the Witch . . .]
I learnt to sit perfectly still
Evangeline
awoke me
to the sound of reverb marimbas
bouncing their kinematics
off the shaven wooden floor

I sensed her scent
in the ductwork
her breath quickened
to the heptatonic ditherings
of ribbon-tied gourds
[—*thought you said "mullet"*— sneered the Witch]
my eyelids flashed
burn-ins of the Aleutians
seen from space

Valverde / Milan November 2006

13

it hacked into that fat blue vein under your tongue hooking in
with claws while eating all the meat it cuts off the blood so the organ withers
once it has eaten your tongue it stays clamped to the stub & speaks instead of you
Evil Goats Terrorise National Park *local residents demand culling*
quartering & grilling with onions 'before it's too late' said someone who
wasn't there in the present climate it would be deeply irresponsible
not to speak in Securicrotch cliches as we roll out more rafts of blended
opportunities for mixed-sector partnership the personal freedoms
which have been referred to by someone subsequently thrown out of the
scout hut
were acceptable once but this is now & it's threatened by
at least 300 goats in the Nantgwynant district of Snowdonia:
damaging property vandalising gardens & undermining
the fabric of civilisation not to mention the washing line
& engaging in practices with outsize knickers draped over their eyes
which cause offence to all right-thinking persons & preclude satisfactory
communication with the locals these beasts persist in playing
chicken with all the passing cars we've reached a point where it would be
a dereliction of duty not to call in National Trust marksmen
to cull the most troublesome some of which have three foot horns
& alien pupils we owe it to our children
to shoot the goats with the yellowest teeth in the head
in the most painless & humane way possible
I've now lost letters from two of Byron's coevals: Ball Hughes
(*The Golden Ball*) & *Poodle* Byng as well as Niki Vendola from Puglia
a successful gay communist politician though I may have confused
Nik's dates after the fight in Hunstanton town hall
I ended up having a beer with the Dutch wrestler Rough Hewn Cleat
who said his dad played bass with Heinz back in the 60s
all peroxide crewcuts & nail-varnish red Strats:
I'd like one of each for Christmas
Data Rape & Function Creep won the week's tag-team cup
the file frays my edges into the fog
honk & that slight give under the heel in the dark which is
England after rabbits & Mott the Hoople were brought in by the Normans
we got the idea of drafting all immigrants
to bolster our presence in Iraq or whatever it was called
as long as they brought their own mobile phones penknives or spitfires
from Poland Rumania & Bulgaria to ensure a fully integrated

European system   just don't spill water in the glider
how many half-empty tins of household paint can you hold in one fist?
ensure no ice crystals remain within the cavity
blow through the end without legs
Cymothoa exigua enters through the gill of the snapper fish
& feeds on its blood until it can become its tongue
then it can eat things in its host's mouth
the whole body & shoal wagged by something else's
language for a generation

Cambridge / Norfolk   2006

14

I went to ask about those bollard jobs;
they say they'd rather fill plastic mouldings with water
but apparently there are still openings for dab hands with a cleft stick
to locate long lost landfills and recyclable cycles on the canal bed or
to map the coordinates of where wayward supermarket trolleys go to die and nail
small black disks to trees; this one, for example, is Comune di Milano N°. 14909
at least that's what the faceless information desk said adding by way of an excuse
that you can now pay to park your car by SMS,
I wish someone would fax me Emmanuelle Béart I replied
i *Milanes* have all Gonzaga.
The word is out:
a goat-rat pact
a M.U.D.
in the mud
nutrias dressed as Care Bears
and armed to the teeth with tiny brillo pads for adjusting graffitti to make it fit:
"Berlusconi has collapsed!" signed AdverCity Passive
now carefully restored by Little Paws to: "Long fool Frankless years"
a heap of sawn off serifs left jingling at the wall base:
New Roman
ends up as
Faux Wiggly
The little critters craved relocation schemes and a sense of community:
some stuffed putty between their toes for speed of movement
and plunged headlong and newly-finned into the Naviglio
where I once saw a side of pork bob past the Cartiera Binda
roll and catch the light; a glistening City of Lard
others gnawed slabs of the tow path loose, eking out a sort of barge
wherein to stow dreams and other provisions
in view of winter's lateral wipe
sensing the first cold out there somewhere: sharp invisible chrome-clean peaks
under the filthy drape of unbreathable autumn
you might have crossed paths off Chioggia,
paddling your little bit of England,
they are armed with very pistols, they sing their rodent shanties through the night
the rest fell foul of brutally trained folk with unquestionable values
able to inflict the Viking Horn Hold and a Troll's Death
Once the goats-on-a-bender area has been cordoned off, a sign should be put up:
GOATSVILLE

Twinned with
Goget'embreaux
Little Nobbit on the Sly
And perhaps that German fish . . .
G O A T
O
G A T
A T
G O
T A O
G

December 2006   Milan

15

you might like to visit Shrimpton   in her Marazion gaf
a tasty *crab & saffron tart*   then   *brill with broad beans & pancetta*
choc-ice in treacle   according to the Sunday Sport
I'm burning you a classic   to stow onboard your head
my sweet tooth says I wanna
but my wisdom tooth says no
seems half a lifetime since I painted Eve
stumbling through allotment gates   her fig wrapped in a soft yellow pad
of withered rhubarb leaves   *Bending New Corners* seemed to whisper
through her p-pod   in my sketches she too was hopelessly drawn
I scumbled powdered milk & soot   into the greys her eyes required
this is neither the time nor the place to claim English poetry
has been insufficiently influenced by Lester Bowie's *Serious Fun*
I remember when I first saw those fascinating maps
of library LP surfaces   deft edgy pencil flicks of recent trips
hiccoughs   scrapes   pissed lunges towards heaven
knows what or whom   a deep trench through *Rigoletto*
as he wandered home in darkness   sarcasm & sweat drying somewhere
untouched between the inside of his mind & the empty night sky
Cecilia felt you couldn't have your cock & eat it   *in a consort of voices*
had a jagged rip which sent the needle swerving inwards fast
a one-legged skater from Marston on acid
speeding straight for the only hole in the ice
the whole question of taste fucked me up for years
as I lisped & ached through lips   bronze-wound strings
& dented tubing   some of the poems are sermons
some stroke purring pussies with bells on in the sun
but all of them are songs
just as all of Bach is dance
but won't be in the morning
did I ever tell you about Cecily?
autumn was brimming with mussels-in-cider
we had radiant lapfuls in warm terracotta   reflecting stars
& a watchful blonde from Finistère   she photographed migrating birds
had to catch the midnight train
the paper glued inside the box lid
showed sparse hieroglyphs & arcane strokes
on an otherwise white ground
drawings of sin on the soul

                                        birds assembling to leave
                                          an improvised notation of improvisation
I sometimes see Maderno's statue in the night   her obsession with virginity
was partly her distaste for knackers & crannies
partly the spectre of the Madonna
but mainly wanting to wake up dead
turned & tuned into nothing but art

Norfolk   December 2006

16

I've been working myself up for the january hoop-dive
by nibbling spelt on toast and coming to terms with the fact
that you can't listen to Purcell on Media Player while you're Googling Ms. Béart
the horns get stuck impaled
a sync-less
three-second loop
of Laswell
redoes
Pinnock
which I deal with by hard-wiring a copy of *The Metro Poems* for Win98se into the last available slot and get off at Trastevere, even though Giulio Agricola is my stop
all I can remember now is her hand still fallen
half off the plinth.
There is no sign whatsoever of Maderno on the 7.30 metro
no reflecting stars for Cecily on line one
it's all slag and bone
got up earlier than thou
or sophisti-tart faces on disposable rollers for late sleepers
bent on sparking workplace
backspace teen muff fear
among bleakened males
remember when you reached beneath and cupped it in your hand?
The first time
is like the last time
and all the times between
so when seconds before being peeled off the tunnel wall forever
the Max girl strokes her isoperimetrics through sand-blasted denim hipsters
I shoulder my coo stick, stuff the Neil Young songbook *sottobraccio*
and start looking round for an opening
a stairwell
the browser crashes
and Purcell picks up
it's the Witch's messenger scene:
Mercury's goat comes clogging in on Blakey's
to Lee Morgan playing *A Night in Tunisia*
He's going to make a lyre out of me freaks the tortoise
Belinda tries to reassure him by saying that you can't screw Texas Specials to a lute
but even a handmaiden's wrist is useless now that we've got Floyd Rose, a couple of Laneys

and some Eric Sardinas bar-code tabs for bendable tetrachord
so I put on my sailin' shoes
flick the vallecular rim of my travelling hat
and head for the coast
surf's up! quips Mercury
get up offa that thing
                                        says Dido
Dance till you feel better

Milan   January 2007

17

Sam, what readers do we have aboard?
Only the one, Sir.

I sat with Blake's *Thel*   which messed up my decasyllabics
& recalled a gentle modal grope on E   [Dorian]
            I reversed through the gloaming with Zoot Sims' *Doggin Around*
        redolent of the last local outdoor festivities
    a rusty Christmas tree flat on its back in the lay-by
      her beds were unpicked brillo pads of twisted thorn & briar:
        a waist-high summer wilderness of green curved air & wire
the pillow slips she stitched by hand throughout the month of May
now hanging   in the Lowestoft branch   of *Help the Aged*
Berlioz said that for the revolution you needed
four brass bands: one to cover every exit from the church
                                        when you finally get the boat back into the water
                                the wood should swell & close the gaps below the waterline
                    but this will only happen if you believe that it will
it's easy to see   you're still feeling muff-
                        led   the old romantic jammer
            with a bent & tarnished tube   full of ancient pains & trains
                        a Yamaha Silent Brass System   stuffed up your bell end
                        partly   but not exclusively
                        for the sake of the neighbours
one lead from the trumpet-mute   to the black box on my belt
the other flows from the holes in my head to your box babe
you might play out your heart for years with no-one listening
            sitting with a lapful of warm chips in a dirty Vauxhall
            cheap malt vinegar two fingers deep in the see-through bag
remember when you reached beneath and cupped it in your hand?
            who would have thought that guitar bridges could span such distance?
                    now I know that Blake's fourteener wasn't just a conker
  I can listen to Tom Waits' *Orphans*   go with the flow without counting
but dreams still scrape my stubble   the harsh translation issues
stir with a big knob of mascarpone & grated nuts
woke me in simmered sweat at three in the frozen morning
  also known as physics
  Régine Crespin sang   the six summer songs by Berlioz
  hours or years before we all become the ghosts of roses
  tell me where you want to go   *the unknown island*

it's a turning off the A14
some charts are just a broad expanse of blue with meticulous legends
    depths are in metres & all bearings are true
        the Krewe of Endymion wasted hours
            throwing sugar at the folk of New Orleans
                before ducking out of the rain for soul food:
                    a piece written   over the chord changes   of another
                    is still a contrafact   many of the networks evolved
                    in the brain are late music the colour of dark red wine

Norfolk   January 2007

18

Schoolyard penis seen from space!

I'm in the herb department of Castorama
side-tracked into looking for a boiled-wool spliff satchel
a parting gift for the Witch
let's go breathing in the humble grass
I also need the gear to leave in the sense of remove my own verdant mark
on Monte Calenzone by night
the piped music twirls me round and I feel the lure of this encrusted Ottoman weed-siphon
which is the dog's bollocks, shiny as tope, and the colour of nougat floating on Redon seascapes
the hang-tag is crammed with tiny tips like: *creosote the underbelly of a seabass before wall-mounting*
I want to try fly fishing in Alto Val Staffora
it's mainly for the poncing around in thigh boots and braces
or perhaps chest waders, which invade the physics of the pool
beyond your wildest dreams
cast up your gaze:
leave behind the city sky's faint grey grip on pale balsa
the barely audible clacsons at the back of your mind
may serve to push these half-mountains slightly back together
though you will never quite get to save the Amaryllis piled in boxes outside the florist's kiosk
do you think I might have met Thel under another name?
January flickers and the screen goes Windows environment blue
you speak of fourteeners, and trombones which can be raised in unison
or dive and roll in flying ace solos
when F-valved, certain arrangements crave unlikely melodies
a turnaround in C for bass clarinet
prepared mangle
my kite guitar
and your new trombone!
primming with silence and soft sheen
sliding its access, producing suckboot curves
your bracing strut is hard work and Trombone Arm conceptual grounds
for Italian percentage disability pay
underarm hair fatally roll-on matted
reduced circulation conceivably due to pit score clamp

jobs you can do with Trombone Arm:
/hard discount supermarket bouncer/ /transversal plumber/
/golf caddy/
/fledgling/
jobs you cannot do with Trombone Arm:
/photocopy monk/ /seamstress/ /pied piper/
/soul sculptor/
others horny jobs:
/radio ham/ /plight analyst/ /fig cupper/ /floogle/ /dragon snapper/ /ship's carpenter/ /codpiece muse/
/mystical fish handler/
/late-night bongo wizard/

Milan February 2007

19

a creature with its eggs between the words

small lights shine across the bay
  from the direction of Wrangle or Old Leake—
in the absence of a New York bridge
  I used to practise trumpet
in the phone box by the lighthouse
  but it's harder on trombone:
now the glass has gone
  the sound insulation isn't what it was
but in recent bouts of fog
  I've prevented several shipwrecks
& prompted two new local legends
  regarding the transmigration of lighthouse-keepers'
incessant moaning
  the sand & salt get everywhere
under your flaps & scouring in your slide
  I've seen the barn owl solo down the Stiffkey road at dawn
you have to stop & tongue the light
  wherever you can find it
1½ ounces of Selmer Tuning Slide & Cork Grease
  sort out most problems
just drip some in your *sugo*   smear it round your rims
  but watch out if you rub it on your chest
like Vick's & then make love:
  I rocketed for the headboard
with the pace of a Ducati
  & no goggles or helmet to hand
unwilling to answer civil questions for a week
  I just wore dark glasses & slid the Voodoo
Trombone Quartet in the Walkperson
  why do you think the Spartans camped
wherever their Mascot Goat sat down?
  & after Otho was dethroned in 1862 can we really believe
that his successor   William George   Prince of Denmark
  was picked by Olivia Newton-John who then forgot to tell him—
so he only found out he was King of Greece
  from a scrap of newspaper that wrapped his fish sandwich?
I'm having *astakomakaronáda*

as it rains tables & chairs on the terrace
putting cubic kilometres of sea mist in my ouzo
DVDs of elsewhere can occupy decades
& only last week the rain stopped for hours:
these dunes dried in a southerly breeze
& my mind briefly lightened like the sand
tipped whispering off the edge of itself

Norfolk   February 2007

20

I bought a fish
and called him Chipset
I made a tank
of crooning gleam
and held him there
belly posed on waters' palm
his fish parts shone with usefulness
he had a clear need
we did experiments
explored together
the man-fish interface
he called me *dull-skinned one*
I told him about our troubles
he made a fish frown
and swayed as if to shake
his neckless head
he hummed me soothing bits
of Harold Budd
after a few
we sang hits from the '70s
for air guitar and burble
he marvelled at my shaved scalelessness
and called it *wisdom*
he felt the lapping closeness
of the world that water brings
I knew the tank was too small for him
and for my long rogue wave
of imminent sorrow
so I sealed the house
waxed frames and keyholes
spun the wobbly taps
until the searing rush dulled
beneath the surface
after that his questions drew closer
less stochastic
he asked about wheel clamps
food in chains
and why at times
he felt so heavy-tailed

I bit the greying rubber
of my trombone snorkel
answered through my cheek bones
then reached below
and cupped him in my hand

Milan February 2007

21

*Conforms to BS 5889 type A**

Paul Klee's dog salutes the 21st tree then heads towards the duomo
via Bar Magenta in search of Buddhist chub the German name escapes me
on a pre-unit Triumph/Duke hybrid splintering the top of the garden fence
so what do you think I say to the absent mystic name *I should do now?*
the new trombone is only in my head with lime & ginger sinusitis
"I see what you mean about Manu Codjia's solo on *The Point*" says Heine
"he do chuck all his kit o'er the ditches before jumping don't he?"
I see us in the dusk outside my window surrounded by nothing but air
I scuffed the rhubarb badly in the move: I dug it up [plus trumpet mouthpiece]
like Cecilia's unchanged body but then a bit fell off each end
I called in the RHS chopper from Wisley: the air-ambulance came skimming in low
the lift was made & inside a minute we were tilting fast forwards over trucks on the A14
against the spin of the Earth's rotation the vital organism stashed in a Russian doll
of hi-tek boxes towards the perilous Brandon Creek passage
way out on the haunted Cambridge/Norfolk border:
I planted out dismembered rhubarb in a waxing moon with stomachfuls of horseshit
to rheum music: *Watch What Happens / Shadowland /*
What A Little Moonlight Will Do / Blue Moon / Blue Room
& crucially *It Never Entered My Mind*
I recall my own disjointed journeys
changing trains in Paris at the age of 16 *en route* for nowhere but the night
or sailing from England on 28th September 1983 to escape from the clanking
that turned out to be tied to my tail then that drunken drive from Rome
to see the sun rise up the side of Gran Sasso or Lynn & I dumping the car
by some salt pan then walking all the way to Cadiz
I planted one by the compost heap one in the middle of the vegetable patch
& one by the laurel hedge with an orange washing-up bowl upside down on its head
I've also been doing some geography & find we're gently being worn away
slowly tilting down towards the east as the sea laps up to lick our laps
they say the view's improving it's important to keep playing as live as you can
I've been strumming this tune about Armide for the best part of an hour
damp curtains hang on the step-ladder drying as new paint dries on new walls
we sold that house full of dead skin cells & the smell of discount Dulux
& as I strum some ghosts do shuffly jostles between the window & the bushes:
Dvořák Gluck & Handel Haydn & Jommelli Lully Rossini Salieri
the witch made us do it they cried she put this peeled willow switch in our hands
& the moon rose over Yeats & the roof-rack I never asked to be in this position

me & a local kipper hung out to dry during a rare break from winter rain
someone stole my St Christopher to chop cheap coke up on the dashboard
I jacked up rusty cars with my chest   it was only my breath that kept them there
the witch's demon rodents fed from my pockets
yet from the car's disconnected speakers   *A Dance Gittars Chacony*
will modify the Earth's magnetic field & change the colour of our eyes

* *except loss of volume on cure*

Cambridge   March 2007

22

Motionless cranes exert a firm hold on what is clearly out of view
I set about unpicking the sounds of this by practising first on my goat's wool muscle shirt
meticulous bits of coat hanger return it to its previous state
as this happens I wonder if I will ever unlearn this lack of technique
by simply introducing patterns: wool-teasing downloadable threads
which necessarily lead to rummaging
and in this case a quite forgotten bottle of Roero Arneis:
since when, Hughes, was wine supposed to taste like mud?
The label exalts the suck-stone of bobbing pumice Eno green
serve chilled with On Land in the discperson
while paddling in the murk chalk flint shallows of the Tanaro
You and Heine are right about Codija:
he does have a way of handling burst length into sweep picked tone slab removal
selected points chipped out at speed analog twib noddling
weeding astutely out the para from the noia
to leave the usefulness of crusts in the acoustic soup kitchen
At first I thought this insidious whirring might be spring
playing hell with my optical nerves doing away with corporeal conductivity
the Witch had a thing about battery-powered regalia
Giving nature a helping hand she said trapped in clasps and harnesses
as she bonged the entire stash of deep-sea sherbet
come to think of it, Evangeline had scute-like toenails she tended
in short skirts with a coral rasp
then there was Armide's tempered mask
and Dido sea-watching
though no tails to talk of only distant painted roundels
You see, we don't get many mermaids this far inland
although one once beached on the (in)explicably drained Naviglio Pavese
I've heard she now works evenings in the hypermarket
her bar-code reader a sort of metronome
drawing hapless shoppers
their plastic baskets unstabled by rolling bottles of Menebrea
they clasp this month's Men's Health with a pull-out-and-keep
on how to use your dick as a scarf next winter
on cold nights and spring mornings
with a pounce in your step
as you head blindly for check out number 22
with milk-free milk and a cellophaned bundle of shards

heraldically   (in)explicably   clutched
but weren't you already in the supermarket?
That's mermaids for you
it isn't what they do
it's the effort they make you make

Milan   March 2007

23

"today's the day I'm gonna grab my trombone & blow"

well   you might have known Thel   as Koi Spice   the timid one
who wouldn't leave the sunken wreck to sway into the light
flooding the wide roof of the ocean   her eyes sometimes opened too wide
& she always kept her top on   which murmured *Mermaids Rock*
but I think it was just her address   she never sang to strangers
    or followed her imaginary ships up unfamiliar estuaries
                she played it safe   which perhaps is wisdom
                but you can taste the desolation of her final days:
                just buy a little jar in Castorama   – *Koi Spice* –
a bland beige dust that merges in with backgrounds
        tasting like wine made from finely-filtered mud
I think you'd prefer paprika lime & ginger pork with Grechetto
      followed by creosote digestivo that shivers & kisses your timbers
      meanwhile I put the same old Analfabetti Spaghetti   chilli flakes & lard
into my broth which resembles the canal where once I contemplated
starlight kissing bobbing pigs – waiting for them to flap their ears
patter the water with their tiny trotters & rise into the sky like swans
   Nicolette Larson on backing vocals drifted over the waters from some bar
       as I watched from the shadows of Viale Sforza
even the letters waited in vain for the mix to turn tidal & ease downstream
to cast lunar Adriatic spells on the last vestiges of winter
& wasn't it in Corsa Porta Venezia that Wolfcarrier
           designed that hall for stars
it all seems reassuringly familiar yet distant
                          Orfeo heard about the death of the soul & it didn't feel true
                         so he went down the dark track of song
                       to look carefully under his hearing
                     the shadowed singing changed his surroundings
                   like radioactivity   heat   or   gravity
                 thus his soul was returned to his presence to take back to surfaces
           as long as he looked ahead & sang   but as always some thunder & bluster
       bothered the tunnel & ear canal where echoes off
     lifeless matter seemed to jar & sneer
& he turned to make sure his heart had actually been working –
 wasn't it Tolstoy who said that happiness was like water in a fishing net:
 lift it up in front of your eyes for inspection & it's empty –
                                        nurse it along behind you & it bulges?

I've popped a book by Peter Riley in the post
& two beet tops for Mrs Pina's goat
now I'm going to find out more about stone
walk on   walk on   with hope in your heart
don't forget the milk

Cambridge   March 2007

24

Whales surface in Tuscany

The last audible sound was the slab blubber heave
the wet towel slump of washing from the drum
last thoughts of true grit and ligaments
hills under foot rose around the aching curve of bone and bones
while backronyms populated lists with the crashworthiness of love
    so I'm having a pint of O'Hara's in Ittolittos
with The Barbarian and we get talking   at least I do   about The Mermaid Problem
and the pros and cons of Vibrolas on SGs
Andy has a tattoo of the Aleutians seen from space on his forearm
it bends like a Floyd Rose as he drains his glass
    we agree that the mermaid at the checkout
ain't exactly La Zemanova, though she does clutch the keys
to all four chambers of our hearts
her fluke thump messes completely with my echolocation
to the point that consciously breathing
I end up beached on   or perhaps   in
this Tuscan field, all gelled up with nowhere to go
                                        thar she blows! gagged the Witch
                                        fusiform forearm fore-wipe
                        a sleeveless wrist bone trap of weird silver bracelets
                the leash of metal in hot weather
her ash dye tramp stamp   an arched
    brocaded   koi   framing
                addorsed regardant squid beaks
                                a cornification device
we set out to scan the shelves for Draughtflow and chitins
but I am hopelessly drawn to a Bluetooth jaw hands-free kit
with Velcro three-day stubble attachment
suited   the box says   to whale-speak
bile duct tape (included) will help remove
an airful of wireless bycatch:
MMSed screen shots of Geri in keratin shorts on a pod racer
hindered with Spice tunes and repetitive tab
        ambergris necklaces
                chagcha ringtones
and if you hadn't called me on a land line
I would text you a wisp of this mud-free Friulian Burgundy

its widely acclaimed memoir-retrundling qualities
enhanced by silkworms
who lit the slipway
          the land-locked gape
                    of the last Leviathan yawn

Milan   April 2007

25

Mare che fiumi accoglie

Veronika was hopelessly drawn to Tom's smothered chops
you're the only one here not chasing tail   she crooned
    (which wasn't   strictly speaking   true)
    as she eased herself out of her mermaid costume
making me spoil the track by overdubbing 2 & 3 on 1
    l'angelo nero persuaded Schwanda the Bagpiper
to pork around with trollops   smoke in public places
tinker with strangers' appendages & duff designer trinkets –
even blow down the end of drugged octopuses
  reworking maritime ballads & blues-inflected shanties
  into glistening yards of slightly twisted spawn
      his soul was as stuffed with sin's fat roe
      as an infected gap in the head with bright lime mucous
      full of the salty tang of young sea-lettuce in spring
one day   poised to abuse a beached whale at Brancaster
Schwanda was saved   by a mystical German sea creature called
the *Omniscient Mussel*   sung tonight by Jill Grove (mezzo)
  Schwanda der Dudelsackpfeifer
  let me tell you pronounced the Mussel in gritty German
  you are coming to a sticky end   as usual
  having a whale of a time
  but dribbling your prodigious gifts into the sand
  you're giving skateboarding a bad name too
fuck off said Schwanda breathlessly lighting up a Camel
you're not even in this opera   *it's just poetry in motion*
    yet Schwanda was given another chance
      & returned from hell without that natural backward glance
        I myself have just been practising   modal shifts
          & have tipped the spit   out of a student model
            (soprano)   it's the end of an era
              this could be the last time   I don't know
Helen didn't even go to Troy
she spent that decade in Egyptian resorts
doing yoga & aerobics
Tai Chi   organic gardening
the odd poetry workshop
auditioning for girl bands

& snuggling up with Menelaus for counselling sessions
today we're doing the history of the mind
a bit of distance learning   Kurt Vonnegut said
we're here on earth to fart around

Norfolk   May 2007

26

Since echoes come from different directions than the main sound,
They may be ignored more easily with two ears.

So there's me and Childe Harold sitting at the kitchen table
waxing lyrical   though it's mostly wax   about our ageing Lolitas
and how you start out with a cough
and the next thing you know   you've got opiate alkaloids
taking fragments from the day's dealings and pasting them back into dream
there's a greased joint to which weeks get universally screwed
   the complexity of it all runs past you in seconds:
a handful of hand-picked gravel tossed on the soft tin roof you cower beneath
another   puffy   metal storm sliding in on seamless   (in)visible runners
                always only just above our heads
rain's rising static is defeated by the chugging of this original 60s nebulizer
which I methodically charge with broncholdilators   gin and isotonic
a Marsh Chapel remake: the entheogenic potential of aerosol
        it seems to work because I'm hopelessly drawn
            to this slightly skew whiff iron-on jpeg of the Mayan calendar
              on Evangeline's half top left to dry in the microwave
                          did you ever notice how much Chiccan looks like a mussel?
Just then Tom De Quincey pops his head round the door
strikes a sort of Friedrich First Light Pose, and says:
                    see how obsession crashes into life   hangs   then disappears?
                    It falls through a previously unnoticed opening
                    a   lidlessness   you'd never really sussed or seen before
                                the machine stops
rain refills the tiny shallow tray of (immediate) silence
a cough punched into kitchen air   resonates   picks up something in the dish rack
                          a bowl   the rack itself
or else the case of Morellino down the hall
carelessly shipped without cardboard dividers or the slightest regard for form
   clutching my auditory illusions lab report kit
which assures me that all over head-sized sounds are diffracted   if not   scattered
   I reflick the switch
         tumble back
              into the foul vapours
   it's an awareness level thing
these sets of tracks are yours and mine
from time to time they coincide

what you expect is what you get:
early morning power-shag
the breakfast of champions
the once over
I am what iamb says Harold

Milan May 2007

27

Aphrodite, riding on a goat keeps me here, anchored in song

I'm still removing yellow hopes & memories from the loft
finding things I thought were only in my head:
the mask & snorkel Lynn used when chopping onions
a video of Frankie Howerd's 1973 sitcom *Whoops Baghdad*
(followed by the shadow cabinet apparently
making seasonal treats for dogs from sieved liver & advocaat)
my old croomstick scorched by Jenny Burntarse
the pickled dick of some Venetian saint
2 boxes of almost-fossilized fishing tackle a derelict French horn
w*hat does Byron think* said Shelley
about the Sudan goat wife death scandal?
well Charlie seemed to really love his goat Rose
to the extent that a bunch of Sudanese elders
had to force him to do the right thing make her an honest goat
& pay a dowry of 15,000 dinars (£25)
the marriage didn't last Rose seems to have died
after swallowing plastic wrappers on the mean streets of Juba
Byron with a fragrant Italian countess sat on his face
was neglecting to think about it at all but when pressed
suggested *oh Charles thou art sick* in a deep sweet muff-
led growl there are too many texts in my face today: The Secrets
of East Anglian Magic / Welcome to Tehran / Mastering Mullet /
Norfolk 'n good: an anthology of Norfolk Modernist Poetry/
How to Really Sell Your House/ *check out*
thenationalmulletclub.org advised the Omniscient Mussel
fresh in from Kropotkin Seamount before drawing back a curtain of
snot-green seaweed to show Poseidon picking up his prong & suitcase
full of Rilke & walking away from the last blue room of all
even ignoring the cast of Stingray except to ask the fish-arsed blonde
are you the Brighton Marina? [where I got my pirk & muppet rig]
Some god! she mouthed *he doesn't know about the 3 billion acres*
of American ocean *to go with their 2.3 of dry land*
he thinks he still has some control I found my flounder spoon
& a red German jellyworm on a 12 inch Ziplock whisker boom
a small chemical nightlight known as *starlight*
that trembles on the tip of my rod in the dark
as the night river moves out to sea when nobody is watching

we do what the scissor sisters say whispered the O.M.
the world is your limpet in the witching hour before high-tide
I go & try to read the water

Cambridge / Burnham Deepdale May 2007

28

If you think real hard, maybe we can stop this rain . . .

backlit
shelter ads defeat
normalised bundles of early light
spun through rain cloud
giving way
to a deepening
sense of fluid
time-stamped halfway up your heart
is the shambles of trance
and those many corrugated Hoover tubes
leading nowhere in particular
are carrying deft messages of vitality and sin
The Truth Bunny
is out there on the vast sloping verge
her huge gaze set towards the sun
The Tooth Fairy
dangles her bare legs
from the armrests of the dentist's chair
she checks her palm for milky lists
fingering furred game
her fatal apparel keyed
to *amori strani*
I once arrived in Brighton by butcher's van to find you pushing a piano up the stairs
the Abercrombie quartet filled an entire decade with openings
long song
sea swell and fleck
the rough-shod
vinyl notes rose
rise still now
wrapping my horse-head fiddle in vinegar and brown paper
I crouch in morning traffic on the number 91
the bus has LCDs
but no internal guttering
rain-slop swills form(s) soups
waxed tickets skid and slide
discarded   forward   jog
all this   doesn't take   nearly as long as you think

next time we're in Rome we'll have to visit Gregory Corso
    and The Lads of course
        our pockets stuffed and clinking with Nano Ghiacciato

Milan   May – June 2007

29

crotchet=80

a midsummer night's fair gift of airglow
fills the sky with the patience of pearls
the world's a city full of straying streets
whispered the Omniscient Mussel   rocking
in a shallow phosphorescent pool
with a straw in a bottle of *Tamarisk*
I accept a salty   green-fringed mouthful
then get back to my tale   not that it's news to the O.M.—
so after 3 days throwing up in Siracusa (water poisoning— Midsummer 1980)
I catch the night-train to Agrigento   [Dorian]
carrying less weight   & with another page bleached clean in my head
I arrive after the last bar has closed
& wander southwards from the city
until I find a broken orchard wall:
& slept on Earth   too near a goat   & manger full of stars
I awoke to the silhouette of a dog facing east   & sitting next to my head
stirring when I stirred   but with a dogged calm
we shared Parmesan rind   & stale soft crackers in the dark
as another dog ghosted in under the trees   & then another
& we set off to reach the temples by dawn with a pack of 20 happy hounds
(plus Shakespeare   fruit & Durrell   in the bin-bag from Messina)
we arrived before first light   the Temple of Concord   or Demeter
[or whichever mother & daughter invented agriculture before that weekend]
temples remade by changing light in an air   which held wild thyme
in years of breeze from off the sea   I looked over my own shoulder
& although my view was overseen   I saw enough
to leave a sense of rising   *small boats lifted on a long swell*   forever in my head
& a piano beached on the landing
what might our dying Norfolk neighbour want before the end?
we swallow a few more bitter drops
which drop into the deep dark river
that carries us away –
reassurance that the photograph is still under his pillow
his old oar still planted in the vegetable patch
a fork just smeared with red mullet stew
a tea-spoon dipped in retsina
help to reach the bedroom window
so he can look down into the garden
where his old dog sits looking the other way

Norfolk   June 2007

30

July winds heave
disarming
end-of-summer tang
sweep night storms in
flush distant city's sins elsewhere
it does make sense to gaze
to rifle the clear sky for signs
smoke trails cut to
gradual sheets of life-light stretched
sped sparingly proportionate
the aural undertow
enters my newly-mown field of vision
where a murder of crows
have been pissing about
for most of the week
a safe distance from the plough
far from sky and all its stars
the sound is caught up
in one end row turn acoustic trough
where the share forces
the barking of gulls breaking shells
bivalves cracked at dawn
on patchy Margate camber
the hollow wail
of the Omniscient Mussel
lost little ones
smashed to bits
day after day
at least these rakish crows
just tear root stubble
from the ground
with pointless unkindness
at night Callisto turns circadian
cartwheels round the valley
hill darkness softens sleep's steepness
reduces the crows' percentage of black hell
for what they done
Shiva shrugs holds back a wink
ingress to where my nerves won't reach

Valverde August 2007

31

Attended by two fallen angels and an evolving mollusc

in the absence of a nozzle for the old green garden hose
I once again succumb to wrinkled pink thumb cramp
fanning ghostly rainbows at the beans & rhubarb
turning through glistening arcs of soft wet light
towards the disused lighthouse & the west
                    swooping swags of mist
slowly settle on the seedlings
& the midweek nymphs depart:
diverse birds emerge with expressions like mad pirates
seeking beakable earth after the dry spell
we regard each other sideways
as the sky turns farfetched Catholic mauve
filled with aching Bruckner endlessness
the spacious clarifying dusk sung by the first few evening stars
daily vastation   after tea   a dry fly cast into the silence
where any weight there is is in the line
                        it's been a funny month
I swapped that tarnished tenor sax
for a scuffed black ocean-going canoe
& we found out how much is closed
with the help of new maps including OS Explorer 250
constructed on Transverse Mercato Projection
Airy Spheroid   OSGB (1936) Datum
                                    a deer & her fawn at TF670283
so we stood motionless   gently watching each other
 breathing   like in a nature poem
but not the one I wrote yesterday:
alpen/alpen/digraph cluster/I felt sadder/after lunch
maybe I'll change it today as we had bacon
            the Omniscient Mussel is relaxin'
     in a creased slate-coloured shell suit:
  wassup purrs the benign bivalve
hi OM   I say *why have they barricaded Gipsy Green?* [TF691424]
  the local suits heard the goat-girl was coming replied the mollusc
the lost & visionary goat-girl
with her unsponsored songs of tomorrow
                        at the end of our walk
we saw the road from the other side

TF677421   August 2007

32

—Have you ever seen this stone in the chemist's shops, the beautiful and transparent one, from which they kindle fire?
—Do you mean the burning-glass?

G-clamped parabolas reach out with poise
into the constant low-range stink of un-sewn sky
an open seam of fleeting sense
the hitherto
and unswapped code
raise(s) compatibility issues:
how can you get a Mortality Pang so early in the day
with nothing (un)achieved or as yet undone
hauling as if weightless a laden reminiscence into view
the unexpected deep-reaching lymph of regret
sadness pulls to the left
splits the day's harsh fluviality
wide open
twilit rehashed overlays press dawn light
to walls poured from creased tins of authentic space rubble
wilting roller blinds leant squeeze box bellows shot and left for dead
in the midst of this
I shed the skin of sleep
and unable to face the tangible discomfort of city travel
somehow remain within the platform's
flat fag-butt fleck
of bum-sucked stubble highpoints
on the un-cultivatable dull-stained asphalt slab
poured once (only) into this shape it holds
and from which there is little or no escape
I'm going to be late for work
for the rest of my life
no more able to pump up the tyres of the urban cycle
to shake off the dangling offshoots of temperament
accumulated in side-view self-peeks
of irrefutable coarseness
yet overwhelmed on the collective stalk to the stairwell
by YA suits OTG in clever shoes
authenticity seekers with laptop satchels
ploughing through and appropriating

pre-*Autumn* which says the stationer's window
Is a season of ideas
 the tram's bagpipe brakes heave a brazen fart across the
 waking world

Milan September 2007

33

armed with just a pasty, & a chocolate orange
I climbed the Sugar Loaf, & then the Blorange

how long have dedicated Christmas shops been around
& how many of them contain lines as good as
please don't pull string out of the hamster
it beats advice to poets
from websites/workshops/
distance learning programmes/
poets-in-the-community schemes/
backs of cereal packets/
competitions/creative writing seminars/critical friends/
W.H.Smith's creative guides/
which proliferate
& I just thought I would check with
you Marsh
as a critical friend
to see if you agreed
that these examples are just wrong
1 poems should be written only under a waxing moon
2 if you turn your poem inside out everyone will think it is a new one
3 if you don't use punctuation in a poem all the birds will fly out of your garden
4 any poems north of Watford should not be left out over winter
5 poets whose work cannot be understood immediately & entirely
by anyone past the age of puberty have to pay a congestion charge
6 the artistic mass of a poem is the number of alliteration features
times the number of assonance features divided by
the average number of syllables per line
7 the poem is a spiritual doorway & you fall off the last line straight into heaven
8 poems can extend your penis by at least two inches in six weeks
9 if you don't recognise a poem it is probably foreign
& should be detained for months so we can all get used to it
10 once poems have been defrosted they should on no account be refrozen
11 prunings from poems should be recycled within six months
& can stop weeds coming up at poetry readings
13 the closer poetry gets to music the less likely anyone is to be able
to find a spare set of strings

14 poems can be burned in most multi-fuel stoves but the ashes should not be used on the skin even on Wednesdays

15 never put anything in your poem that you wouldn't put in your mouth

Norfolk October 2007

34

perched high above town with the Slag-Angel
we're listening to some Charles Ives
overseeing the sick plies of metropolitan beauty
caught up in the rigging the grief knot
the search for the grace she has fallen from
we exchange our fears in glances: blasphemy clipped plumes snapped shafts and pinions
all that stuff we never should have done or dared to dream to do
she repents the kicks she got in car commercials
lending wings at parties certain film appearances *sotto le feste*
not surprisingly there is wireless on the cathedral roof so we Google *advice for poets*
and get sped to InflatableCrate.org:
poems should be written only under a waxing moon
if by dividing the last 2 digits of the year by chance multiplying the result by 11
adding insult to injury or the day of the month and subtracting 4
you still don't know if it's safe to make the poem
try counting the veins on the splayed backs of moonlit fig leaves
if you turn your poem inside out everyone will think it is a new one
apparently this only works if you use one of the following fonts:
seamless 66 Fay New Roman recobbled MT or sheriff sans serif
the artistic mass of a poem is the number of alliteration features
times the number of assonance features
divided by the average number of syllables per line
there is a formula called CritTOOL in Excel which will help you do this: =SUM(PO1.EM14)/Muse
it seems the macro can be downloaded at WWW.Shelley'sConstant.com
the poem is a spiritual doorway & you fall off the last line straight into heaven
walking the Arcadian girders of the trussless sky I lost my fucking keys again
poems can extend your penis by at least two inches in six weeks
Edmund Spenser
once poems have been defrosted they should on no account be refrozen
redirect to IMDB: a surprising number of films touch on frozen poetry
plot keywords: fish couplets / poultry in thigh boots / tied to bed of lettuce / beef dripping / back to front / performing rights / deforming wrongs / codskin notelets / windy bench grapnel
prunings from poems should be recycled within six months
& can stop weeds coming up at poetry readings
sponsored link to the Bosch COMBO TWEAK-N-JIGGER: churns out excellent poem compost

and makes *everything louder*
than everything else

Milan November/December 2007

35

the immaculate collaboration of tongues of light

sounds like thunder over Titchwell
Leonard Cohen *I'm Your Man*
Christmas watching You Tube clips of bands
local to distance Keston Sutherland
& Stephen Rodefer live in Miami
eating liquorice allsorts
The Mountain Goats live at Amoeba
the hinges on the boathouse door rust shut
during this period parts of the roof quietly slide
into shallow water gleaming over soft silt
we worked away from home for years
stepped gingerly over our own souls each morning
to buy a patch of land to die on
I've never even been here
3 in the morning
an arm around me all night long
the moonlit harbour wall
an empty bottle on a rock
the star's reflection
floated on the sea between her fingers
we didn't know we spoke English for years
we manhandled boats back in the water
like in a children's film
Jean Baudrillard died in the spring
his carbon footprint fading from the world
while flowers made love out of sun
we made love in the disabled toilet behind the Kandinsky
& ideas rippled through the internet
to nest on hard-drives
backing up behind the eaves
it will cohere said the beard
& simmer in the upturned skulls of strangers
I walk back from town out through the woods
across the salt marsh on unmarked paths
through total fictions
dogs may bark but the caravan moves on

Norfolk January 2008

36

Because water is not perfectly transparent, almost all sunlight is absorbed in the surface layer . . .

from the high sill in Villa Goiosa
reverse stone creaks of thunder
seem to grind and wipe
then fade pulled back
to form smooth pleats
of sound drawn in
absorbed
a lo-fi sign of signal loss
and yet beneath
this vertical downpour
Nature sits perfectly still
Her proxy glistens
that's how I know
I've missed my cue
perhaps it's poised
out there where ripples fan
and spread mid-water
once purged
the weather forms
a doubt awareness scheme
rain retreats
light pans out
enters lower down
the grey scale slides
disclosing tucks of headland
until at last
the coast makes sense
revealed woods rise vertically strewn
as if dabbed on
at best unrolled
we crouch beside the rim
the lake itself skimmed smooth again
only determined hysterical watercraft
leave white ribbon rips
briefly taped to a shifting gash
in darkness

January 2008

37

dogs have no pores & polish up well

stitched inflated dog skins
bob upon the water
fixed to nets which drop down deep in darkness
barely sensed boundaries of nothing & knots
4 in the morning & I couldn't brainstorm or sketch
a neckerchief for a ferret
let alone new pastel suits
for the slinky boys of the papal guard
something trundles past the window
no-one says the congestion charge
will keep riff-raff jalopies
out amongst their shacks & ditches
but not much is said these days
build me a cake-stand of Carrara marble
¼ acre should do it (except at Easter)
it must be delightful to lean 18 stone of aristocratic largesse
on one's elbow & look at the horizon with one's eyebrows
everybody thinks everybody else
knows what to think & it's too late to check without sounding thick
easier to buy an apricot poncho
or green rubber duck shoes
just like the ones in the ad
the ones the countess wore last autumn
when the generous sunlight piled gold in every garden
for everyone who could afford a garden
the sun soon goes down
flailing round the cosmos in its brilliant agony
its mad & final conflagration
it's a one-off
a depression of cloud condenses to the west
where the last fish turn & surge towards the nets
those stumpy black buoys glint & tremble in mashed white water
when you touch the boundary
change its shape as much as you can
the dogs are dancing   *the dogs are dancing*

Norfolk   January 2008

38

the Witch sat up whole nights bidding for a shag-o-matic on eBay
fidgeting warmth into the duffel upholstery of the chaise longue
its spool heel legs creaked
left note-shaped scars in the boarding
I dreamt
stop motion scenes
another sword and sandal do
all excesses and OTK
you were there [remember?]
we did a crate of pomegranates
feared the homebound fuzz
the damned seed count
much later
was it still the dream?
Hera and Echo
came round for baked potatoes
and a glass of Tagliatella
she did her E-I-E-I-O thing
when day eventually did come to
it was a click through of misty View-Masters
that hand held
vaguely binocular Bakelite grip
at the scruff of the neck
somewhere between dogged and wolfed
the same four notes keep cropping up:
Bowie   Miles   the Gong on the Hook and Ladder
sharp ascending chromatics step half out
lob chords borrowed
wherever you look street lighting is out of synch
low rate bulbs barely bruise with amber
the town's hind quarters
unable to sustain dawn's infliction
the sensory branding
of night
into day

Milan   January 2008

39

our blood is red coral & we build islands over the abyss

sky in a boat half sunk
near a track that curves from Cley to Blakeney
midwinter wind turns tall reeds blond
in breathtakingly synchronised swerving acres
a small scorpion backed into a corner of my mind
past whiny trance anthems & echoing paraphonia
a lorryload of blue carpet off-cuts dumped on my feet
while happiness quietly covered the landscape
like an unexpected herd of reindeer
the Omniscient Mussel uncoils byssus rope
to lasso the starfish that's eaten O.M.'s mum
& to bind it to five rogue dog whelks
then O.M. abseils in sideways on a slipping tide & hisses:
it's galling to be eaten by an animal
whose mouth is also its anus
at certain alignments of the moon & fiscal policy
tiny seeds of pain glisten in remote folds   listen
the man on the roof isn't always Santa
crab canon ensconced in spectral Norfolk music
rats squashed on the ceiling of the church
Sam Phillips singing the places I go are never there
I look down into myself & shudder
Les Claypool trout fishing in Idaho
dry flies impinging on the water hardly more than sky
yet made of socks
don't hook a moose on the backcast
either the light has mysteriously transformed the world
or you've tipped advocaat on the ice-cream again
the goat plays percussion on Duke Special's Freewheel
& the Vitalic flying dogs
stop surfing On The Kop & head for lupercalia
even empty cups elude us
every authentic artist
secretly considers the outcomes to be
inappropriate misleading & reductive

Norfolk   January 2008

40

much
can be slept off
if you are prepared to brave
the primed torpedo tube of dream
the right apparel
a tight moist suit
its zips concealed
beneath the seams
preferably coated
with angel blubber
for additional smoothness
Chipset knows all the vowels
to Stairway to Heaven
he stuck a cartoon fin to my back
with fish lick
and tiny magic suckers
we beam we really do
our brows tipped to brace
the slipstream of happiness
we went on soul errands together
he could spot a weed-world rift at a distance
and steered me to safety
over dinner
I tried to explain Goretex
and mimed the expression
catch your breath
we compared scales and modes
deep into the night
he expressed a slight preference for
Fortuny
and ballroom attire
It reminded him he said
of the way the sun refracted
though the logged watery sky

Milan January 2008

41

Den Tek Nightguard dental protector
for Nighttime Teeth Grinding (Bruxism) now £22.95

the park now sports 'Talking CCTV'
thanks to a £35,000 grant
from the government's Respect Unit
so we can count the moles
& also tell them to stop making molehills out of molehills
who do they think they are anyway
going around being moles all the time
this should stop you speeding too & being drunk
in charge of legs as your dressing-gown unravels
into nine miles of Prussian blue cotton kinks
you follow through a scatter of starlings & showers
driving & singing the golden peaches of Samarkand
running over a small boy band from Holt
park   duck through mysterious hedgerow caverns
all bramble stem & soiled pads of rain-welded porn
it looks as though there's no path to the sea
swallowed saltmarsh clogs the horizon
salt water whispers through your presence
whisps & phonemes underneath your feet & fingers
the sound of remote waves surfing your head
you have a slight sense of how
delicate evaporation is
if you say Aeolian quietly twice
now reduced to £5: this
sensual collection of slow movements
evening rises from the ground into the night by Schumann
all the subtle colours of midwinter Sirius
are illusion   atmospheric distortion/fatal darkness
how fragile   clear   & beautiful they are
how fast we fly while standing on the ground
talc blue mould spots an actor full of promises
worn out velcro packed with unknown pastel threads
you can't count moles on an empty stomach

Norfolk   February 2008

42

Space is curved, the earth is curved, everything on earth is curved

once fledged the day squirts naphtha
pings Swan Vestas bough-wards
its abandoned nest
the acclivity of getting out
everything we have to say
don't you ever sense
you're walking in the direction
of something celestial and needless
while still hopelessly drawn
to the bosom of careering opportunities?
I've been holding my breath all week
to slow synaptic pruning
it's as if this darkness filled with light
a careful intaglio
brings out the Spaniard in me
flipping back through months of script
some scenes seem pleasantly faded:
the gravity-spill of early morning tram rides
the huge hull of the *camposanto* clipped to earth
flat against a feeble forceless blue
gas-fucked and run through
with obelisks hedged in fine brickwork
pulled back from the edge
the cleaned out tank of growing awareness
stockpiled with the daft names we give ourselves
amid undiscerning dreamers who thumb the free press
their aspiration on the fly
is chipped off bits of groupthink
to sort snort and glean
or rip from the base doings of nightless sleeps
open to debate yet lost the New Rich wake
mediatically pissed at the snap purchasers
the sex-needy the ready at heart

Milan March 2008

43

if this door fails to open, stand well back & wait for the wind to drop

two scuffed notes half-frozen in the wind
under the bed   half a minor third
mouthed by the hinges in her cupboard
the other voiced on weathered chimney lips
careering down through my middle
            caked & feathered with soot
exposed to shakes of displaced light
seen in dream after fake dream of the present
where footprints stop & old estates begin
as one note fades   the light gets briefly stronger
it is not impossible to enter some pianos
if you make yourself very small & still
            in the morning you can press
your knee against its leg   feeling voices
all along your personal valley of bones
            long after they've gone
according to Anonymous 4
there lacked a language to fill the spaces
as 50,000 a day died for want of basics
which are here & there   behind the fences
            WTO   World Bank   IMF
best before: see neck
the percussionist grumbled
the fur keeps coming off my beater
            with every day that passed
the moon became more distant from the earth
            claw an awkward chord & shoot
darkening rapids on cumbersome punts
in wellingtons the repetitive stomach churning
is the right hand the fear is the left
Schumann playing late into the night
until her soul & shoulders ached

Norfolk   March 2008

44

one for DTW . . .

You always were one for mermaids
it was in the family:
 economic dealings
 with other dimensions
 water
 the sand beneath
 its contents
the first time I dismantled
my bike bell as a kid
I gained a sense of
the precariousness
of reversibility
I like to think you were hopelessly drawn
to Rachmaninov's second
in The Seven Year Itch
sipping Glenfiddich
from a broad based glass
 far from the vast affordable light
 of Whitstable beach
 of Reculver Towers clipped into place
pivoted by the careering sway of the 5.50 to Victoria
these days you are mainly
catching tides of dream
 a life of lost sleep
where half-awake images
populate patches in the script
yet never quite punch a hole right through
to where I'm squatting in the April sun
 on the sea wall
 beside the tracks
the trip-wire pings back into place
I wriggle slowly into your shoes

Margate April 2008

45

so tomorrow it's off to King's Lynn
1 fit tow-bar
2 have Great Aunt Maisy spayed
3 investigate suede wall art
on speedway themes
we like to stop off on the way
admire the queen's trees
& the bristling fields
where teams of East Europeans
fill vast trailers with tiny things
for other folks to eat
sometimes it's hard to straighten up
George said
stella maris
stella maris
not a good name for a car
a fire-eater at the East of England show
or the last human cannonball in Yorkshire
it's such a wide & enchanted evening
the almost empty beach
touched with the last thin voices
from an endless wealth of languages
addressed to different
dogs & gods
partners & children
a long way away
& now the night tide
covers everywhere
we've been standing
but tomorrow is another day
until we get there

Norfolk May 2008

46

My baroceptors are playing up again
I try to gather in the last weeks but cannot
my head   like yours   too full of lists
which rather than get ticked   disperse
    1. place poem books in robust shoppers
neath the vertical calm of late may rain
this works fine until I find a letter from you
in the copy of Scrins you sent me from Rome
when our sons were very young
and you were hopelessly drawn
to the snow-bound pensione in Villetta Barrea
    2. check emotional bandwidth
will it bear the heart's identifiable tunes
and the worthless code
which says that spring finally will kick in
though it might be early summer
or a hint of searing autumn yet to come
only now it's July in Valverde
where we actually live and
    (3.) succumb to the importance of written light
the spinal crumple of dense green foothills
as early each morning I groove my way down to town
        beyond this crisp back lit ridge
the city's livelihood seems as if whisked away
            in a keenly expressed vitality of abstention
capitalising on the calm that wells inexplicably up in me
                as I swerve jolt and bound
    the caked on asphalt breached
        forms hill scar tissue
          the crops stay still
              the valley slowly rotates

Valverde   July 2008

47

the Omniscient Mussel
who's now received an honorary PhD in Being Here
from the University of Wells: Next; The-Sea
is gazing at the flight of butterflies
& reformulating advice to humans
on growing your own shoes
two Common Blues
dance down among knee
high flourishes of Norfolk August
wings edged with
sooty darkness
settle on blade-grey sea holly
in a scoop of dunes
distinct
but near the intermingling tones of strangers
from Mansfield & Antioch (disambiguation)
Nottingham & Oxford
Margate   Gdansk   Milan
odour of stoat under lunar solfège
bees dozing in the last sweet peas
the Omniscient Mussel
gives sweet liquid clucks & recalls:
the possible places
of articulation
form a continuum
along the upper surface
of the vocal tract
so the places listed above
should be seen
as arbitrary

August 2008   Norfolk

48

. . . and Jungle Gardenia crash on Pine-Sol and beer...

The past has been hacking into my dreams
        bundled with legitimate claims to sleepless nights
I sip coffee as if it were a linking potion
an organic
        short cut
            way out
                into day
                        the valley's bright haze
            beyond the blind
a sort of soft shelter
      from the mismatch
of dream-frames split
    time-set spandrels
                 mind's misplaced –tectures
      traipsed among
re-assumed places and events
                 they trail away as smoke plumes
     from the high planes overhead
starting their long decent
               their mechanical howl
dealing with turbulence
           the reminiscence bump
code culled
                 tapped from the deepest possible vein
   where patching up
        fenestral wounding
             flagging recognition
                 shapes sentimental logograms
                                 of the awareness hope
               that what we write is read

Valverde   October 2008

49

early autumn morning thought
you heard your footsteps
coming back to meet you
the faulty street light clicks
buzzes   & hums a new tune
in front of the Hôtel de l'Avenir
the duck standing just out of sight in the fog
where an empty sports shop still promises
new away kit now available
it's the kind of day
when new people are conceived
by the universe   are born
or die forever   twist the knife
in distant strangers   or enrol on courses
called things like Yoga for Begonias
for a moment it looked as though
the world could be unpacked
from all our damaged cases
& cleared from all these shredded papers
dishonoured contracts
stained canticles
& left out all night to shine among us
luminous mist suspending
a tree's last wet apple
while somewhere electrical
Sonny Rollins
live in Toulouse
plays
More than You Know

Norfolk   October 2008

50

A post-chemo disability allowance of 70%
brings an immense fortune
of handy exemptions
many of which are hyphenated:
tax-free hang-gliding accessories
replacement canisters for sky-writers
artificial limbs *paghi due, prendi tre*
esteem baths [no VAT]
70s disco compilations
excluding *that's the way I like it*
lacustrine cup cakes
ex-RAF wheel chock
stair-to-ramp adapters
walk on the other side of the road kits
plug'n'play *go back to where*
you started from connectivity
spiritual rags to ragged spirits converters
your very own dumpster
Harold Melvin and the Bluenotes
co-ordinated soul-step
dance-floor decals
a low-risk new versatile
acronym disk egg poacher
3 subscriptions of your choice
scuffed faux state-side stylist Asiatic trainers
with names like *brandish* and *dicer*
mp3s of the city's grind
geared to indifference
and everything slightly too dirty for words

Valverde – Milan   December 2008–January 2009

51

Nick Cave is in the house

& as the Omniscient Mussel mused
on Len's pink tights & bristles
it recalled blobs of molten lead
dropped from a height of one thumb
into tumblers of very cold water
making shapes & signs
such as this front end of a prawn
some kid outside with issues
in the glowing Tuscan gloaming
shouts *tonsils are bollocks*
for her own reasons seven coals fuse
in a draft from the forest out the back cadmium
orange thoughts sent fluttering through
the diminishing fuel of autumn fires
the bronze long gone for cannon in Ferrara
it's not too late to start again
red dust sifts down through pin-pricks in the master
buffering now 49% complete
sea-food inspiration &
Aretino's *I xvi modi*
he cut through the old man's skin
to find the empty nest
that death had made there
ah the Light the Pisan
Chips the Beer
the Lightly Battered Haddock
these are just a few of the dance steps
performed tonight on moonlit Gypsy Green

Norfolk January 2009

52

the day John died I dined
on a pint of O'Hara's
shouldered my Strat
drove down
the dull steel
tape canal
to Sound City
where though I feel
the music in my bones
I can't pick out a single tune
he'd slap looped
strut and pranced
in buccaneer loons
a deep wail syllable drawn
and sheered from
his hurt heart's clutter
conjured me up
a djinn on the floor
in the huge house
on the Dover Road
with the gonged and the bonged
the fiercely in love with love
we drank off the swaying sadness
slept away the '70s blues
tonight they surge and waft back in
as Lulin glows green in Libra
and silently sheds
its tail

Milan February 2009

53

'There is nobody here but us chickens'

when Haydn
went to Slough
to see the stars
he tinkered with creation
& explored certain
new yoga positions
like
Feed Wrong End of Dog
Wash Foot in Caravan Sink
& Kick-start the Transit
but in the western ghats
we watch cloud goats
& listen to the notes
almost turning
into solid air
we steel
ourselves
but not for long
sleep-spindles point
towards a club
where you can go
to be yourself
or sit & knit
some little coats for chickens
the bones & mortar
will turn to beige paste
& thick bars rust

Norfolk February 2009

54

love and hate are two horns on the same goat

the Witch is back from a long stint
she is wearing her hair up
as a sign of atonement
she says we can still be friends
she is listening to Steve Hillage again
she calls me the turdy wordy man
after supper
we knock back
chive and spearmint shooters
dwell on the vast potential
of the drinkable garden in general
and why Janet Leigh's
moleskin shower cap
didn't do the trick:
she'd have been better off
with the Vikings
who never quite made it here
reach out though they did
craning their midnight necks
Chipset says the Witch is my *hag-for-life*:
because she is
rewired *to*
the dream-deprived *edge of my*
fish-sleep *she gets her*
hexy *knickers in a*
twist *and clutches at my*
retrievable *soul*

Valverde February 2009

55

(for Rory Gallagher's birthday)

Did you ever wake up with them bullfrogs on your mind?

scrape rust off the wings with dad's wire brush
& light comes through with views of vetch & shoes
where once there was a Ford things get lighter
shift in the wind for the first time in years
as you traded in the organ
for a sunburst strat sat in the yard
where the conservatory was going to be
walked past museums but peered
into pawn shop windows
a connoisseur's hands held behind your back
admiring hip-flasks jewels & duff mics
in the grace of clouds passing deep inside the glass:
his had a battered sheen from sleeping in ditches
spillage & smacking Vox AC 30s
[& a Dallas Rangemaster treble booster]
a '61 Fender improving the environment
adding several storeys to the building
made of misremembered traces
lost weeks drunken knocks blue-black blues
a mix of pegs by Gotoh & Sperzel
disparate pick-ups picked up on the road
rewired tone pots new liver & nut
a wrong five-way selector & warped scratch plate
which possibly brings that neck pick-up
just too close to the sun moon & stars [solo]
& other lights that pop

Norfolk March 2, 2009

56

Rory's Strat did cluck
and bevel sound tapped into
whirring curls note curds
raised in tufts rotating honed
the resonance of guitar wood left out
in the weather's bad temper
on end for days on end
is what some say slowed down his blues
smoothed / soothed until he held
a fist of mid-tone hum clutched firm
then punched against the air
at intervals he eased / released
whatever it was inside
and what if every sound we ever made
            is never really lost
but fades forever imperceptibly halved
until it forms part breath part nudge of light
                                        the twinkling plain
                                          a bay of amber ships
                                            glimpsed through
                                           a pale new-born
                                         rolling oily lens
set halfway up this huge glass
hemmed by winter's last grip
and spiked with headlights on the ridge
they burn then turn then fade ellipsed

Valverde   March 2009

57

as many had foretold
aliens landed on Dartmoor
in teapots formed from multi-coloured lights
& early Hillage solos
they beamed through to rooms
featuring chickens with four legs
Hughie Green's parrot
Compo's ferret   a giant armadillo
The Great Mexican Trilobite
& a band of stuffed guinea pigs on the sherry while
knocking out Kenny Wheeler tracks
on tiny tarnished instruments of brass
dead rats gamble for fake cash   squirrels sip port
& a bunch of moth-munched rodents play cricket
near a church made entirely out of feathers
the lifeless remnants of albatross
coypu & lamprey mingle with
badger traps   French milkmaids' yokes
a Tasmanian convict's cap   & this pixy made
from bits of lobster
the O.M. knew they wouldn't hurry back
even though they'd missed the best displays:
Kittens' Wedding   Death of Cock Robin
& in the staff kitchen   the non-stick
flat-bottomed wok

Devon   March 2009

58

Corso di progettazione del suono
(Frequenza bisettimanale)

Now that the magic has gone   I drift around the Cinque Vie
every other archway hides   a full-blown strip out
rubble cupped in unexpected   space and light
heady scent of *rustin negàa*   lethally mixed with moped No.5
and after an hour   I end up at a table
where perhaps we sat   in Bar Magenta
and though it's barely 9   I weigh up the consequences
a celebratory pint   reminisce then move on
afraid to let go   tired of the day-long trade off
the bar is familiar   but I don't remember
the betting booth   the Red Bull chiller
in the far corner   what looks like
the *Scrofa Semilanuta* digging   a full Meneghin breakfast
while outside traffic   is building up
church front beggars step back   into pre-morning's last opening
giving way to couples   with ipods ideas and morning routine
they step out arterial   their monthly swipe card ins and outs
now consultable on the intranet   since we outsourced the payroll
just about as far as it would go   to the huge angels opposite *La Borsa*
they look down chipped   worn wings weathered faces expressionless
the buy and sell   the freshly minted iron lung of greed
betrayal trashing   this town's long since spent rebuildable soul
office centres for future generations   of flying fuckless by-passers through
who never felt this long breath of   history   exhale and settle preening on the plain

El nost Milan   April 2008

59

Minchia, che bella!

Lynn's made ginger & rhubarb muffins
as gifts for the Spring Oracle   spongy
sumps of treacle rising up towards a new moon—
the oracle   (which actually prefers
Norfolk Pork & Haddock Chowder – a tradition
accidently launched last year)   ordains:
throw away your watch strap
place watch on tongue
& shut your mouth
fortunately
we have kept a few for midnight feasts
& share one with the O.M.
esconced in a birch-twig cabin
the size of a fist or heart   up in the Magic Willow
[see *Quintet on St. Cecilia's Day* for more details]
the O.M. – now snug in a muffin – mutters
let the moon grow out of your heads to fill the sky
& change the sound of the wind with permanent readiness
for seconds   as the earth turns in its sleep
& a city drops to its knees in the dust
a few fleas settle back down on the stray dog
by a fountain in the dark piazza
the sun will burn out your eyes
unless you project its power onto paper

Norfolk   Pasqua 2009

60

Chipset is talking me through Data Grief
he calls it *Unreinstatable lossfulness*
the hard drive clicked
hummed inaudibly soft
and locked me out
what's worse I'm left with
a searing abrupt vulnerability
intended encounters
conversations rehearsed perhaps for years
kept somewhere in mind then lost
no longer accessible appropriate   or simply set aside
this could be why most nights
at 2am half my head erupts
as if something were boiling
beneath the skin it cannot broach
in an attempt to lighten up
we prise open a couple of bottles of Forst
Chipset tells me *why do . . .* fish jokes
(. . . because haddock is the past tense of havoc . . .)
and reminds me of the time Evangeline
took one word right out of my mouth
I nearly veered off course
again and again and again
why asks Chipset do we say *under*water?

Milano   May 2009

61

blown breathless a
on the ragged gradual
edges of the present intuition
in my new loafers sings
& Petrarch hood through
I lunge out of clifftop gales the vision
& slip into haven of distant
with a large bloomer Spica
& a four-pint tub in Virgo
of milk-free milk to the south
the O.M. says Laura holding
is a dream of social justice an ear of
as well as bright eyed wheat
& bushy tailed Persephone/
in the firelight Astraea
the pagan Avon lady goddess
burrows through the storms of justice
with scuffed catalogues Libra
while the planet teems the scales
with unfed connoisseurs surrounded by
underwater in the sense the lion
of understanding snake
& crow

Norfolk May 2009

62

crow alights on the pylon
at the bottom of the field
instantly explodes with a dull crack
the fireball floats impressively
slowly out of view
                                        at all angles
the other birds waft upwards
then settle on the wire
                  on vertical tips
 of nearby
                dead branches
as if overseeing   the explanation
               of no second chance
watch where you put your feet
   I tell this to the Scrofa Semilanuta
who weeps uncontrollably
   and reminds me of Charles Mingus
in a flurry of retraction
   I try to calculate a path to the pylon
as if to show her that it never really happened
   I've never been down to that crease
at the bottom of the field
   up to now there was no point

Valverde June 2009

63

(1st version/take 4)

the Omniscient Mussel is listening:
hark *Reincarnation of a Love Bird*
& recall how Mingus
could click gummy limpets into the sea
with a miniscule twitch of his fingers
Lynn & I finish Tippexing the plimsolls
ready for the opera at the Fakenham Gas Museum
it's a familiar plot: beauty is stolen by the regime
then used as a model for culture & the Madonna
who oversees & overrides each
twitch & simmer of temptation
from a glowing niche set high up in a wall
dividing this world from the next
a virtual planet refreshing the decrepit
again that aria *hose down my tail plumes*
in a white-tiled room & bake me into Narnia
had many sighing into their vanilla tubs
Eric Dolphy buzzes the current on bass clarinet
Paul Bley colouring gaps in the air soft & loud
Mingus restringing the actual pylon
with live cable & plucking a lament
for every bird no longer on the wing or wire

Knapton June 2009

64

new balcony poem

Chipset and me have been out here
for longer than I care to admit
the outmost beam has turned
all the planks sprung free
they clatter when you walk
toss tall pots of green enamelled basil
here and there at every step
so we sit as still as we can
and watch the combine
nibble at darkness
its invisible feelers reach deep
into sequinned night
its flood lamps light long trembling cones
they trundle out of sight
leave behind a soft incessant cake-tin howl
as if the valley were a sort of bowl
emptied out retaining only sound
through clipped waves
Nature exhales reaches out
with no words to speak of
set against this out-blot
of olfactive stars

Valverde   July 2009

65

zuppa di cozze alla tarentina

the Omniscient Mussel
was rinsing its hinge
in a thimbleful
of Pedigree
& listening
to a Jackson Brown tribute act
called Snow Patrol
an oar enters the water noiselessly
disentangles a knobbly stir of weed
pushes a wobbling dimple
back into nodding & dazzling plain
every mind-map becomes
sandcastles after two days
& nights out in the rain
I resume
my distance learning
course on absence
management
by evening a thin
skin forms on each
idea & shivers

Norfolk   July 2009

66

I'm comin' up so you better get this party started

down in the village August comes bundled
with the Radio Zeta sing-along
melodies shaped amid vaguely heretical fumes
of herbally enhanced *salamelle alla piastra*
the sausages' replete wafting fills the air
with swirling pork-mementos
searing top-end sizzle
static for an instant filtered out
by the two-prong mutra
the tune itself is stripped of frequencies on its way uphill
arriving as a glib muffle of sentiment and croon
and just as this starts to feel real
the breeze gathers down the valley
fans it all elsewhere leaving trills   creaks   blips
each more distant   or closer   than the next
nightscape's depth of field restored
severed only by the spooky pulse of landing lights
and yet the stars seem set flat against the sky
Venus is both yours and mine
another day has gone
at any given time   we raise our separate glasses   triangulate and grin

August 2009   Valverde

67

that's one of the places yetbutaswell

it was Beethoven who first observed
the road to Rotterdam was paved with chub
well it's not cramp & it's not flamenco
I just lay my burden down
& someone picked it up
& ran out of the station
you damn right I got the blues
though the bushes now lean in
with more than a Hint of Mint
& the Vauxhall Astra Green
which haunt the season's magazines
    it is true that in our younger days
we were meteorites over Burnley
but now anonymous visitors
have to rattle a poker around in our mouths
when it is time to start the day
so many August stars have plummeted
from the windy darkness between
Perseus & Cassiopeia
since I first took Leonora for the coalman

Norfolk   August 2009

68

"Through Music, time is absorbed into religious expectation, since the instant is immediately open to eternity."

after blanched aubergine skins
tossed in raw onion
and balsamic vinegar
I feel somehow invincible
bathed in the fumes
of stick-around permanency
gathered beneath the fig tree
I know what you mean
when you spurn attempts
to stir summer's slighted
off-cuts into
autumn's minute abandonment
loss bound by
transitional gain
there won't be stars tonight
although
the turkey rissole moon
will light
the sinusoidal sky
till dawn

Valverde September 2009

69

It's a bit like when you point at something
that you want a dog to notice, and the dog
just looks at your finger.

here in the U.K. they're knitting poems
to celebrate the centenary
of the Poetry Society
& shrews make little partings in the grass
before owls pounce then plummet upwards
to perch in the branches of dead elms
among forgotten constellations
I remember when we met in west Vienna
I had skate
you had the dark Russian sole
we talked about the inabilities of silence
to express immensity or domicile
the separate subclumps of the Virgo Cluster
the need to scratch at the skin
of some tambourine till blood peeps out
the motto of the mollusc: what is
human about humans may be *logos*
but life remains the slow construction of a home
in unspeakable tide & hunger

Norfolk September 2009

70

Periwinkles survive low tide or danger
by closing their operculum (trap door) to the outside.

Chipset says it's
not seeing
the sea
in over a year's
what *cartoonifies*
you perched
then lost
reflected in
the tilde of surf
a strew of
history expressed
as notes
they wriggle free
invade unrolling beach
the trumpet squeak
of bivalve turn
beneath a thinning
simple gash
of sun

Valverde October 2009

71

Perhaps I eat to persuade myself that I am somebody

a long procession ambles past the window
to mark the golden age of Norfolk art
which begins each evening
at about this time
out in the autumn night of deft
inequity & stars the sky cradle echoes
to many grey & white appliances
another Mannheim Rocket
& reruns of Popeye Doll
wedged between the shipping forecast & dim news
eggs on the boil rock knocking in a dented saucepan
through a mysterious smell of Swarfega & lime-pickle
o season of radio halos
it's as if Heine were just around the headland
trolling for zander & listening to
some local country music
from the days of Tory happiness
when donkeys wore high hats

Norfolk October 2009

72

On Margate Sands I can connect nothing with nothing

lead came window grid-
 mapped pre-
  dawn sky from Red Sails
   as if the house itself
    had turned night in for soul-
     flight over Minnis Bay's slack water
      intertidal rumble strips
       now thickened in October sun-
        tint townscape screen overlay back-
       dropped back and weighed
      against vast obedience wherein
     we glide along the Esplanade veer
    leeward at the Nayland Rock
    where only practical cats take shelter
     from the intemperance of haggled verse salt-
      dried spring rolls fading honk
       and the limitless unoccupied space of everything
sensed unsaid now anchored bobbing at the Outer Tongue

Margate October 2009

73

una sera cosí strana e profonda
che lo dice anche la radio

it's well after midnight
as the final trucks
heave the last of the Fair
from cliff-top mud
to the sound of Lucio Dalla
bonfire roots pulsing in a S.E. wind
oystercatchers stare from outside
a hovering disc of orange light
& then it's the dog zig-zagging
down the garden
too busy & early
for a busy early morning piss
that finds it
in the vegetable patch
mucky & malnourished
with clingfilm wrapped around
the raw stumps of its wings

Norfolk November 2009

74

"I'm never going to get out of this world alive"

all this talk of otherworldliness
stirs pith and ancestry
cloud reverb on cadmean dawn
oyster shells in bleach
Hank Williams sound brands
5am moon tugs at shallow sheets
of rainwater left behind
to bear night's reflected seal
a contiguous clutch of stars
though I can't exactly hear voices
it's definitely heading that way
musical veins pressed
to gauge the viol's drawn pulse
country chordophones
overspent on sin
Cecilia beats the beat of time
counts her fingers on one hand

Valverde / Varzi   November/December 2009

75

what to you now are eyes
in nights to come will be stars

now the pickled onions are fantastic
a first bite twists the spine 20 degrees
anti-clockwise with left shoulder dipping
so folks developed language & language
developed people which helped us knock through
but also dumped too much weight in the boot
thus fucking up most front-wheel drives & those
who squat in the backs of caves wondering
what star-light might be like in ideal worlds
instead of smacking fat pigs with ping-pong
bats from which the rubber mat flaps free or
licking Swindon nymphs in the fairy-light
lit gloom of St Cecilia's Day where
Purcell no it's Mahler is humming you
mustn't enclose the night inside you you
you must flood it in eternal light

Norfolk   St. Cecilia's Day 2009

76

Happy birthday, John Abercrombie

Chipset notes
Mahler's beamless
loft of sky
quietly hewn
from torrential rain
& anchored slipshod
to Earth's off-centred girth
it's my turn so
I stare as far as we can
beyond where the jazz is
to warm tucks of
magnetic heat
coiled round
hollowed out melodies
daylight flickers
and is gone

Varzi December 2009

77

I'd like to do a little more wrong
at this point.

winds aspirate with ice
from hearts of darkness
west of Ely
twitch the old moleskin slacks
as night swallows day
& decades of fen —
over a flask
of magic-mushroom soup
the O. M. admits that this
is as good a time as any
for me to realise my ambition
to drop-kick a warmed-up
chicken & mushroom pukka pie
with my bare foot
for the purposes of divination

Norfolk December 2009

78

a night of hoodening
& the S.S.L slumps spent
in the back of the Honda
pen drive stuffed with dubstep
Lassus De André
the sampled chant
of two softly swaying hags
tucked in the nave
with the Ox & Ass
mesmerised & bodiless
their murmuring fades
these darkened walls
where damaged souls brush through
en route to supermarket brightness
& shrink wrapped trays of Lithuanian veal

Varzi January 2010

79

God does not play snooker

the Omniscient Mussel is fresh in
from a gruelling tour of my pizza
& is sporting a perky Boy George hat
that may soon be catching on in Norfolk
in the middle of the seafood spiral
there is a path down to a cavity
in which a liquid xenon target waits
for more detailed news of the universe
even in the shadows of cheese & caves
there is oppression of a talc-tipped kind
echoes of dead voices coming in waves
to smother & silt up the expectant mind
even in a night of cold rain I sense
something more than water in the water

Norfolk January 2010

80

For Kenny Wheeler's 80th Birthday

horn notes pegged
 to long hewn
  stems fleck silent   air
   smooth spathed metal
     teasel chords unstring
       a knotless townscape
         bracteal & improvised
         flush long melodic flurries
       taken up &   snagged
     until they snap
   colour-coded veins
  implant slack &   rootless
 polished blow-balls
in the blustered   sky

Varzi   January 2010

81

honk if you've drunk from Kenny's cornucopia

invisible harmonic rain
bows arc beyond
our ken a whinny
of despair to crack panes
we're up to our knees
in breeze buckled echoes
of Schumann & wondering
how you say
flugelhorn in German
it can get through the hedge
without rustling
& flick a little ripple
in your lake

Norfolk January 2010

82

"Come in," she said, "I'll give you shelter from the storm."

I don't dream anymore
or turn the trick
majuscular darkness
sleep brain's part-work
a limen posed
I once read I swear
it said a glass of Lethe
tightens resignation
yet stubs out the day
not that it matters
since what this bus
ram-raids a-sway
is night

Varzi February 2010

83

ideas about diseases of ideas
drift home from the paradigm shift
hide slivers of a broken bell
between the boat's timbers
with apps to propitiate the jumbies
rowing towards the edges
out over the site of floating markets
past the sunken cages where we learned
to click our fingers underwater
a gibbon climbs the last stilt
of a rotting pontoon to show us all
the length of a fish it once nearly caught

Norfolk February 2010

84

"Too much, the Magic Bus"

The Witch flips   through SteamPunk
on back seat   vibro-stink upholstery
tight worn   inlays crave
the colours of   off-road hogs
night beast   radio patrols
cranial nerve   songs unforgotten
from meek   hark-back years
wafting   & funambular
she tweaks   her funicular cincher
l'amore   she says is
the miracle of flight   *the fainting room*
her chatelaine bears   my dangling name

Varzi   February 2010

85

the past reduced to spicy paste
you squirt around the mouth while reading
teach yourself tantric gurning   the ballet
set to notes of light with singles
doubles twitching through the HD pin
pricks on black packs of pilchard
flavoured crisps & shapely schooners
of recycled cider plunge to hours
adjusting wire & fake cargo   beep
ballast helps the craft float to her lines
& nights of phosphorescent wake

Norfolk   March 2010

86

tiles of
primary brightness
cast in
muntin shadow
a tattered map
fallen
at my feet
whenever
we were lost
we held
each other's breath

Varzi   April 2010

87

north Lynn Duende

I have dusted the stuffed weasel
& placed it in a sunlit niche
tinged submarine by stained glass
made with patience & the urine
of prepubescent redheads
in centuries & minutes gone by
even the O.M. is sleeping
rocked in whispering sea-green dreams
spasm of tangible absence
rose & broken into cold song

Norfolk April 2010

88

Chipset my Media Dragoman
says sound & vision will do me good
 he toys with a set top decoder
allocating bandwidth
to ghost masked flaws
in the wireless ocean
of fandom & tears
  I gratefully prepare
 fuddling cups of clam dip
laced with entry-level Armagnac

Varzi April 2010

89

antiphonal
Ambrosian
it will soon be time to end the preparations
O Spanish bluebell girls of Galway Bay
O little tin of Tanglefoot think 25
cashier confirmed over 18
wtrcrss spinach rckt
a stately procession passes the back of my mind
change

Norfolk   April 2010

90

then you must have heard
that heron rising
scapular
rice fields
brim with sky
transeptal chanting
slowly floods
its allocated
stave

Varzi May 2010

91

even before the goddess
of love & her
horny henchpersons
eased the bamboo sliver
through the tough kebab chunk
of my heart
I glimpsed others sneaking
to the woods for fuel

Norfolk   May 2010

92

Aphrodite did like her hubris on toast
thunder rolling in on sky bleached
clean fluff caught
in the retiary whisps we'd set for bats
and wayward spirits wrapped
in freefall through whatever they use for air
only to bounce to a halt
on the softness of the world

Milan May 2010

93

David Chaloner *Collected Poems*
didn't he & flew some in my life
o little grebe slide sideways by
on what appears to be the surface of a river
my bird is my wand
I think I'll say that to the memory
of David who is in the zone

Norfolk   May 2010

94

a plump jay scuds ahead
leaves additional light dipped
cuts a deciduous wedge
evening soaked in limes
heavy with the fuming oils
of tree sex flashes magicube
blue & is gone

Varzi   May 2010

95

here's one of you on duffed-up strat   playing the piazza after dark
dirty bulbs swing Festa dell'Unità   through fumes of bonarda
hog-roast & dopecake en croûte   tall Italian night shadow dances
whereas this one has you tugging   on a bell-rope in a tower
still collapsing slowly into   earthquake zone
here's one of me pacing the edge   of my technical area

Norfolk   May 2010

96

badly-welded spring snaps free   of winter's healed crust
my hopes dashed   I shed layers & adapt
a flurry   of weightless   gems
the breathless malaise   of allergy & loss
though storms do go   the stolen echo drenched
no reason to beauty   in un-let blood remains

Varzi   30 Maggio

97

today is indeed the night
the bailiffs repossess the circus
my shamanic jay-suit
comes back from the cleaners
distances begin to fold

Norfolk May 2010

98

Mnemosyne helps dismantle this circensial world
ritual segments   the unbearable whole
she buys me a pint   we stare out to sea
our infinitely infinite numbers mapped
to curves of shells flipped over on their backs

Thanet   June 2010

99

the OM snaps my tooth-pick & buries it
certain fadoms under Old Hunstanton beach
            the goat-girl & diverse demi-muppets
      are gathering to do the dance   farewell

Old Hunstanton beach   June 2010

100

Chipset says   this bladder of hurt within
holds substance   thicker than tears
blessed with the will   to float   or sink
                                        or tread   thick limbo

Thanet – Valverde   2010

101

it is time to suck the tender sticks of Stockbridge Arrow
dipped in tangy latin sherbert
& redraft my translation of Handel's Green Prats

Norfolk June 2010

102

last poems   tied to the mast
a gentle push   we settle back   alone
kelp shadow   stuns the air

Thanet – Valverde   June 2010

103

we'll meet again   for Jameson's in jam jars
                        at the end of of this unadopted road

Fakenham Gas Museum   June 2010

104

once the well-tempered musics are worn thin
we'll still have the clinking gift of goat bells

Valverde June 2010

105

just time to pull on the feathered leggings

Norfolk June 2010

106

& swap love for light

Valverde June 2010

www.ingramcontent.com/pod-product-compliance
Lightning Source LLC
Chambersburg PA
CBHW031150160426
43193CB00008B/322
* 9 7 8 1 8 4 8 6 1 1 7 1 9 *